# Webpack for Beginners

## Your Step-by-Step Guide to Learning Webpack 4

Mohamed Bouzid

Apress®

## *Webpack for Beginners*

Mohamed Bouzid
NA, Morocco

ISBN-13 (pbk): 978-1-4842-5895-8        ISBN-13 (electronic): 978-1-4842-5896-5
https://doi.org/10.1007/978-1-4842-5896-5

Managing Director, Apress Media LLC: Welmoed Spahr
Acquisitions Editor: Louise Corrigan
Development Editor: James Markham
Coordinating Editor: Nancy Chen

Cover designed by eStudioCalamar

Cover image designed by Freepik (www.freepik.com)

Distributed to the book trade worldwide by Springer Science+Business Media New York, 1 New York Plaza, New York, NY 10004. Phone 1-800-SPRINGER, fax (201) 348-4505, e-mail orders-ny@springer-sbm.com, or visit www.springeronline.com. Apress Media, LLC is a California LLC and the sole member (owner) is Springer Science + Business Media Finance Inc (SSBM Finance Inc). SSBM Finance Inc is a **Delaware** corporation.

For information on translations, please e-mail rights@apress.com, or visit http://www.apress.com/rights-permissions.

Apress titles may be purchased in bulk for academic, corporate, or promotional use. eBook versions and licenses are also available for most titles. For more information, reference our Print and eBook Bulk Sales web page at http://www.apress.com/bulk-sales.

Any source code or other supplementary material referenced by the author in this book is available to readers on GitHub via the book's product page, located at www.apress.com/9781484258958. For more detailed information, please visit http://www.apress.com/source-code.

Printed on acid-free paper

*To my mother for her unconditional love and
support during every moment of my life.*

# Table of Contents

# About the Author

**Mohamed Bouzid** has over a decade of experience in technology and web development. He studied programming and graduated as a software developer and then later became a system administrator. With a humble beginning, he started freelancing from home – providing services to people around the world. As an entrepreneur and project engineer, his work today is mainly focused on solving problems and making products that people love and use every day.

# About the Technical Reviewer

 **Alfred Myers** has been interested in computers since he got his hands on a magazine about digital electronics back in 1983. Programming these computers has been paying the bills since 1991.

Holding a dozen Microsoft certifications and being awarded Microsoft MVP in C# for five years in a row starting in 2007, he has recently been educating himself on open source technologies such as Linux, networking, and the open web platform.

# Why Webpack?

The very first question anyone should ask before using any tool is "WHY?" Why do I need it and what's the benefit? If you have almost no idea about webpack, then big chance you are already asking these questions, for me, the situation was that the framework I used to work with decided to switch to webpack for the assets/JavaScript management, and as result I found myself struggling to understand how webpack works and wondering how to make the switch to adjust my code accordingly, if this sounds familiar to you, this book will help.

In the following introduction, we will discuss a little bit about why webpack and why you should even care about it. If you are looking for a quick answer, it should be this: your JavaScript development will be fun and much easier! Too good to be true?

I admit, I wasn't a fan of webpack, and the reason was that I never took the necessary steps to learn it or understand it. In fact, I was taking the wrong approach, trying to copy snippets from here and there, or looking for quick answers on the internet to find out why my JavaScript compilation failed. Mostly I was stuck for long hours searching without moving ahead to what I was supposed to be doing. During that time, I started to notice other people complaining about webpack, asking how to install this or that, and why their preferred third-party libraries weren't working anymore, especially in the world of web frameworks. It was a shared feeling, and to be honest learning another Javascript tool wasn't a fun option, so I kept myself stuck until I changed my mind. That's when I decided to figure things out for myself, which has led to a long journey with webpack, but if someone had handed me a book like this one back then, without any doubt, it would have saved a lot of time, frustration, and many hours of trial and error.

JavaScript is becoming more and more complex, and if you have a big project or app that will someday grow to a certain size, webpack will eventually save your day (we will see how over the upcoming chapters). One of the main things webpack will do for you is to compile your JavaScript to one file or more. For example, you can have two final scripts if you prefer to call one JS file in one page and a second one on another page.

Compiling your JavaScript into one file will prevent multiple server hits. Let's imagine you are using many third-party libraries like jQuery, Tinymce, Bootstrap, Loadash, and so on.

Instead of calling each one separately like this:

```
<script src="/assets/javascripts/jquery.js" /></script>
<script src="/assets/javascripts/tinymce.js" /></script>
<script src="/assets/javascripts/bootstrap.js" /></script>
<script src="/assets/javascripts/loadash.js" /></script>
<script src="/assets/javascripts/some_other_library.js" /></script>
```

You can put all your third-party libraries in a file vendor.js and call it in your HTML with one line:

```
<script src="/assets/javascripts/vendor.js" /></script>
```

The same principle applies to your own JavaScript files. Plus, you can add a hash string to your files name to bust cache and to reduce your site/app time load. Webpack has you covered.

Is this all that webpack will do for me? If you have ever used another build tool like gulp or Grunt, these tools were already doing this and doing it really well. All your JS code, for example, was concatenated and compiled into one file with a hash string as well (for caching) and life was far easier. However, have you ever thought about global variables and collision when concatenating multiple files into one and how they can cause a problem if you don't use classes or wrap every file's code with an Immediately Invoked Function Expression?

Well, with webpack, all these problems are solved out of the box for you, no need to reinvent the wheel. Also, one of the features I like most about webpack is how it will manage dependencies for you, and decide which file is necessary to load before another one, etc. I was faced with this situation in one of my projects and it was a huge pain to keep track of every file I needed to load, and which one depends on the other so that I can have them set in the right order. Maybe you have a small project right now and you don't see the benefit. But as your JavaScript keeps growing, you will see how much benefit webpack will bring you, and you will be thankful that you made the right decision from the beginning.

That's not all. Webpack can also manage your HTML, CSS, IMAGES, and other files like fonts (via loaders and plugins). I think the best way to think of it is like a manager of your assets. If you ever visited the webpack official website, you probably have seen the following image.

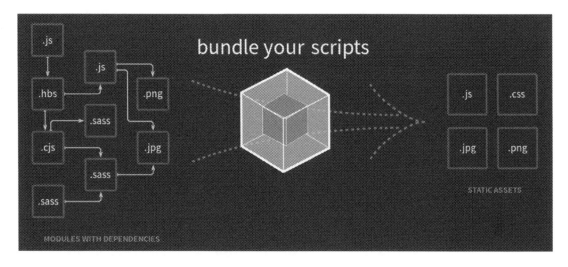

*Source:* `https://webpack.js.org/`

This illustration shows how each of your files (on the left side) may have one or more dependencies (your files could be of different types like png, sass, js, jpg, cjs, etc.), and how webpack can take care of them and turn all this chaos into one or more organized file(s) to serve your assets from.

Webpack can do a lot more than what I have described so far, and we will see the many things you can do with this powerful tool through concrete examples in the following chapters.

Webpack is a vast subject, and there are always new things and improvements being added to it. My goal is not to cover everything about it but to help you understand how it works so you can use it in your daily work (probably with your own preferred web framework) without having trouble understanding why things are done in a certain way, or why we use this loader, alias, etc. In short, this will help you to stop saying, "I don't know how it works but it works!"

Another thing to know (as previously mentioned) is that most web frameworks have adopted webpack recently for building and compiling JavaScript; and if you are using a framework like Symfony or Rails etc, you may find that webpack is already configured and ready to use out of the box. This alone is a huge win if you had to configure it by yourself, but in order to use it, I believe that you need to learn a little bit about the configuration and how loaders and plugins work. Once you learn that, you will be able to see a very clear picture of how things will be used when dealing with your JS inside your X or Y framework. So, whether you are using webpack with a framework or not, just trust me on this, and let's learn the fundamentals that will make you a problem solver when it comes to using webpack.

# CHAPTER 1

# Webpack: First Steps

In this very first chapter, we will start by laying the foundation for our work by installing the tools we need in order to run webpack on our local machine. Then we will talk a little bit about the default configuration that webpack has introduced with version 4, called "zero config." Next we will write our first "hello world" example, which as you might already know, is a mandatory standard when starting to learn anything new. Finally, we will talk very briefly about the webpack bundling command that we will use in order to build our final output files.

## Installing Webpack

First of all, you need to have Node JS installed on your machine because webpack relies on it. If you don't have Node installed, you can go to `https://nodejs.org/en/download/` and follow the instructions based on your operating system.

To check if you have Node JS in your system, open up the terminal and type the following:

```
$ node -v
```

The next step after making sure Node JS is installed on our machine is to create our working directory/folder, which we will name "webpack_beginners." Depending on your preference, you may have created it manually or via terminal like the following:

```
$ mkdir webpack_beginners
$ cd webpack_beginners
```

Once you are in the webpack_beginners folder, use the following command to initiate a basic JSON file:

```
$ npm init -y
```

This will create a file called package.json that will save references to our installed modules.

1

© Mohamed Bouzid 2020
M. Bouzid, *Webpack for Beginners*, https://doi.org/10.1007/978-1-4842-5896-5_1

Via npm, the -y option is to answer yes to all prompted questions; it's not that important for us at this stage, so we will just say yes to everything.

If you open the generated package.json file, you will see something similar to what is shown in Listing 1-1.

***Listing 1-1.***  package.json: The basic generated JSON file

```json
{
  "name": "webpack_beginners",
  "version": "1.0.0",
  "description": "",
  "main": "index.js",
  "scripts": {
    "test": "echo \"Error: no test specified\" && exit 1"
  },
  "keywords": [],
  "author": "",
  "license": "ISC"
}
```

The package.json file will serve for NPM to identify our project (name, version, author, main entry file...) and handles the third-party dependencies needed for it to be fully functional. Assuming you are creating a JS library that you want to share on GitHub, etc., you might be interested in changing the name and the version above, and maybe write a description as well. But that's not our focus here, to see more what this package.json file will do for us, let's install webpack using our command line:

```
$ npm install webpack webpack-cli --save-dev
```

Note that whether you are in Linux, Mac, or Windows, the command is basically the same assuming you have NPM installed already on your machine, which is mostly the case if you followed the installation of Node JS correctly. The --save-dev option is to tell NPM that we need this just for our development purposes, meaning that these packages will be installed on our local machine only.

The command above will install webpack for us with its own CLI (command-line interface). Once the installation command finishes, open the package.json file, and you should see something similar to what's in Figure 1-1.

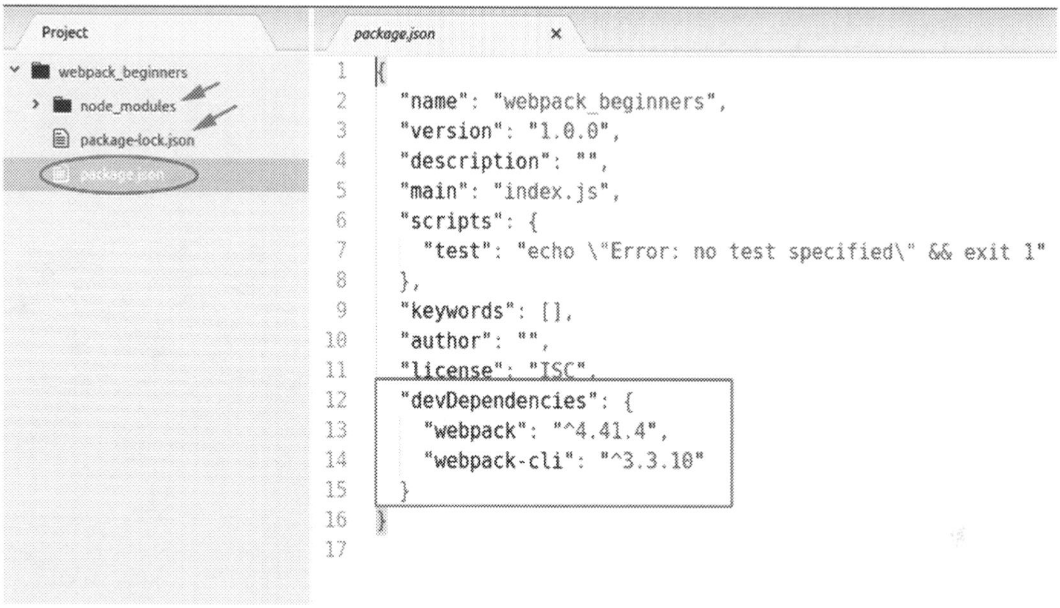

*Figure 1-1.* *The package json file after installing webpack and webpack-cli*

Notice that webpack and webpack-cli were added with each one's version under the devDependencies. Also notice that a new folder called node_modules was created, as well as another file called package-lock.json.

So, on one hand, in addition to the basic generated properties (that we have seen above) like the name of project, version, author, etc., package.json lists all the packages that your project directly depends on, meaning that whenever you install a new package from your terminal, that package name and version number will be added to package.json. The package-lock.json, on the other hand, is the full representation of the dependency tree of your project, including the indirect dependencies. For example, when you install webpack, other packages that it depends on will get installed as well. Package-lock.json will also contain the specific version of each module, so that if someone took your project later and ran "npm install" on their machine, they will get the exact same versions you installed. That way there will be no breakdown on the application (i.e., due to a package that got updated and has some break changes).

Now that we have our webpack installed, let's try to open the node_modules folder and locate our webpack package. Figure 1-2 shows the exact location, which is under "*node_modules/.bin*".

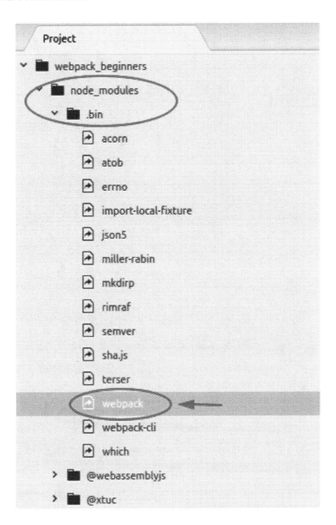

***Figure 1-2.*** *The file "node_modules/.bin/webpack" responsible for running webpack command*

The file "webpack" above (under "node_modules/.bin") is where the "Webpack command" comes from, so every time we need to compile our JavaScript, we'll call this file from our terminal. However, there is a better way to do this (which we will see in the next section) by making an alias command that will call that file for us instead of specifying the path to it. With that in mind, it's time to write some basic code and start exploring the power of webpack.

# Webpack 4 Zero Config

If you ever used webpack 3 before, you know that you have to create a configuration file called webpack.config.js in order to tell webpack where your files are, what to do with them, and where to output the result. Webpack 4, by default, is zero config now, here is the quote from webpack's official website:

> *Configuration*
>
> *Out of the box, webpack won't require you to use a configuration file. However, it will assume the entry point of your project is src/index and will output the result in dist/main.js minified and optimized for production.*

Source: `https://webpack.js.org/configuration/`

What this means is that webpack expects you to create an entry file called index.js inside an src folder, and then it will create and output the result in dist/main.js for you, without the need to create the configuration file yourself or do anything else.

I will assume you are always inside the folder we created in the first place (the one we named as "webpack_beginners"). So now let's create a folder called src and also a file index.js inside it. In Figure 1-3, you can see a screenshot of what my folder tree looks like.

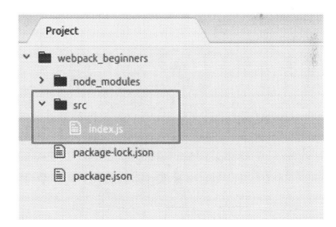

***Figure 1-3.*** *Our "webpack" folder tree after adding an "src" folder and index.js file*

In your index.js, write a first hello world alert:

```
alert('Hello Webpack World !');
```

Save the file, and in your terminal/console, run:

```
$ node_modules/.bin/webpack
```

What we did here is to tell webpack to bundle our JS. If you wonder what a node_modules/.bin/webpack is, it's just the path to our webpack command, which is basically a JavaScript file itself. There is a better way to call it for sure, and we will see this in a few moments.

After telling webpack to bundle our JavaScript, webpack will go and search for src/index.js and start from there, after executing the webpack command in your terminal. You will get an output similar to what is shown in Figure 1-4.

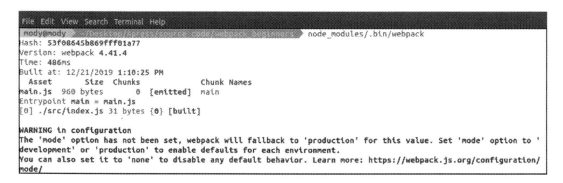

***Figure 1-4.*** *Terminal output of running "node_modules/.bin/webpack" command*

As you can see from the output, webpack specifies what was built for us as a result (a file called main.js); also notice a warning at the bottom that says the following:

> WARNING in configuration.
>
> The 'mode' option has not been set, so webpack will fall back to 'production' for this value. Set 'mode' option to 'development' or 'production' to enable defaults for each environment.
>
> You can also set it to 'none' to disable any default behavior. Learn more at `https://webpack.js.org/configuration/mode/`

This simply means that we haven't told webpack what mode we are working on (development or production) yet, as result, the fallback is set automatically to production so it decides that our JavaScript should be minified. In order to get rid of that warning above, we will add a flag `--mode=production` when calling the webpack command like this:

```
node_modules/.bin/webpack --mode=production
```

After the compilation is done, let's take a look into our text editor (or IDE depending on what you use) and see what we've got in Figure 1-5.

***Figure 1-5.*** *main.js: the file generated by webpack under dist folder*

Webpack created a dist/main.js file for us and compressed our code as well – but wait a minute! Don't you see that our alert ('Hello Webpack World !') transformed to a strange code? I mean that there are more things added to it. Let's wrap the code in our text editor and take a zoomed look, like it is shown in Figure 1-6.

```
main.js                    ×
1   !function(e){var t={};function r(n){if(t[n])return t[n].exports;var o=t[n]={i:n,l:!1,exports:{}};return
·   e[n].call(o.exports,o,o.exports,r),o.l=!0,o.exports}r.m=e,r.c=t,r.d=function(e,t,n){r.o(e,t)||Object.defineP
·   roperty(e,t,{enumerable:!0,get:n})},r.r=function(e){"undefined"!=typeof
·   Symbol&&Symbol.toStringTag&&Object.defineProperty(e,Symbol.toStringTag,{value:"Module"}),Object.defineProper
·   ty(e,"__esModule",{value:!0})},r.t=function(e,t){if(1&t&&(e=r(e)),8&t)return e;if(4&t&&"object"==typeof
·   e&&e&&e.__esModule)return e;var
·   n=Object.create(null);if(r.r(n),Object.defineProperty(n,"default",{enumerable:!0,value:e}),2&t&&"string"!=ty
·   peof e)for(var o in e)r.d(n,o,function(t){return e[t]}.bind(null,o));return n},r.n=function(e){var
·   t=e&&e.__esModule?function(){return e.default}:function(){return e};return
·   r.d(t,"a",t),t},r.o=function(e,t){return
·   Object.prototype.hasOwnProperty.call(e,t)},r.p="",r(r.s=0)}([function(e,t){alert("Hello Webpack World
·   !")}]);
```

***Figure 1-6.*** *Our "Hello webpack world" wrapped in its own module*

If you noticed, our alert is at the very bottom, but you can see that there is a bunch of code that precedes it, which you don't have to worry about or understand because it's specific to webpack and how it makes the modules requiring functional.

The next step is to create an HTML file and make a link to our dist/main.js to see if everything works fine.

Go ahead and create an index.html file at the root of our webpack_beginners folder, and fill it with the code you see in Listing 1-2.

7

**Listing 1-2.**  index.html: referencing our dist/main.js file

```
<!DOCTYPE html>
<html lang="en" dir="ltr">
  <head>
    <meta charset="utf-8">
    <title></title>
  </head>
  <body>
  <script type="text/javascript" src="dist/main.js"></script>
  </body>
</html>
```

Save the file and open it in your browser. Yay – the code is working, and your first "Hello Webpack World" just pops out. See Figure 1-7.

**Figure 1-7.**  *Your first "Hello world" alert*

While this is a very basic example of our first working JavaScript file bundled by webpack, it's time to congratulate yourself! You did it, and you should be proud as you just made your first step in the webpack world. But before we move to more serious things, let's talk a little bit about the bundling command and how we can use it in a friendlier way to tell webpack to compile our JavaScript.

# The Bundling Command

As I already mentioned, before we move on to the next chapter, I want to talk about the webpack command we used before "node_modules/.bin/webpack" as it might seem that it's an ugly way to do it, and for sure there is a better way. What you can do is to open your package.json file and look under scripts, which appears like this:

```
"scripts": {
  "test": "echo \"Error: no test specified\" && exit 1"
}
```

Remove the line:

```
"test": "echo \"Error: no test specified\" && exit 1"
```

And replace it with this one:

```
"build": "webpack --mode=production"
```

So it will look like this:

```
"scripts": {
  "build": "webpack --mode=production"
}
```

In the "script" line that we added above to our package.json, there is no need to specify the exact path to webpack file like we did in our terminal because it will know where to find it. Now instead of calling:

```
$ node_modules/.bin/webpack
```

We will use our custom command:

```
$ npm run build
```

This will look for a webpack command in the node_modules folder and call it for us. Note that you can name your script what you like. It doesn't necessarily have to be "build." You can, for example, name it "dev" and then call it from your terminal as the following:

```
$ npm run dev
```

So whatever you name it, you should call it with its name, but you will find that most people generally use "build" or "dev" in the webpack world.

# Summary

In this chapter, we introduced the necessary commands to install webpack on our machine. We have seen the package.json file and what it basically does. Then we created our first JavaScript file and bundled it with webpack. Also, we explored the entry file and how it should be named in order for webpack zero config to work correctly. Additionally, we have learned how to run webpack command from our terminal.

# CHAPTER 2

# Write Modular Code

We have seen how to install webpack and use it in order to bundle our index.js file. Now it's time to see how to add more code files (like in most real-world applications) and let webpack combine them into one file. Then we will learn how to customize our own configuration instead of relying on the default configuration provided by webpack.

## Separate in Multiple Files

As we already saw, we used webpack to bundle our JavaScript. However, in our example, we used one JavaScript file only. What about multiple (two, three, or more) files?

## Calling a Function from an External File

Let's add a new JavaScript file and call it "greeting.js" where we will create a function "sayHello" as the following shows:

```
function sayHello(){
  alert('Hello I am Webpack');
}
```

To be able to call sayHello function in index.js, it has to be exported from greetings.js and imported into it.

Webpack understands CommonJS and ES6 modules, and we will see both, starting with CommonJS.

To export sayHello, add "module.exports = sayHello" to greetings.js so its contents become:

```
function sayHello(){
  alert('Hello I am Webpack');
}
```

© Mohamed Bouzid 2020
M. Bouzid, *Webpack for Beginners*, https://doi.org/10.1007/978-1-4842-5896-5_2

```
module.exports = sayHello;
```

In our index.js, let's remove the alert code we have written before, and let's require the function we just exported above:

```
var sayHello = require('./greeting.js');
sayHello();
```

Now let's build our output file by calling the build command, which is the alias (we created) for the webpack command:

```
$ npm run build
```

---

**Remember**    In our package.json file, we have specified the "build" command under "scripts" option, so whenever we call "npm run build," it will call the webpack bundling command for us.

---

Let's open our index.html file in our browser and see the result. Figure 2-1 confirms that our script is working like we expected.

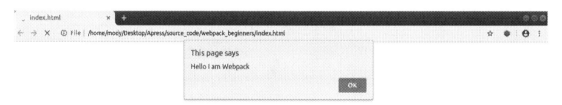

*Figure 2-1.*  *Calling our sayHello function from greeting.js*

Now, let's change "greeting.js" to use ES6 modules by updating our code to the following:

```
function sayHello(){
  alert('Hello I am Webpack');
}

export { sayHello };
```

Then we need to make a change for our index.js file as well:

```
import { sayHello } from './greeting.js';
sayHello();
```

Don't forget to run the build command in your terminal:

```
$ npm run build
```

Then open index.html again in your browser. It's working, exactly like before!

Something I want you to notice here (in the ES6 module example) is that we kept the same function name we have in our greeting.js file, to import the "sayHello" function but if you try to use another name like "greeting" instead:

```
import { greeting } from './greeting.js';
```

It won't work because the "export" is by default exporting the function we have with its own name. But if you still want to use "greeting" for calling our sayHello function, then you can use an alias like this:

```
import { sayHello as greeting } from './greeting.js';
```

---

**Note**    We won't talk about all the possibilities when it comes to ES6 because the main focus here is webpack, but it doesn't hurt to revise some basics from time to time.

---

As we have seen, this is a pure JavaScript way to have a modular code and separate your code into multiple files. But again, at the end, webpack will use its own export/require system when bundling files, which will do all the magic for you.

Also, another important thing to notice is the path to our file when using "import" statement. See that we used a relative path:

```
import { sayHello } from './greeting.js'
```

What if we change './greeting.js' to 'greeting.js' ? What will happen?

Well, if you do so, webpack will assume you are looking for a node module, and it will go and search that name in node_modules folder, not in your source code folder, so make sure to always add a relative path to where your file is located when using the "import" statement.

Another note is that the file extension ".js" is optional in ./greeting.js. Webpack is assuming that a file is a JavaScript by default, so it's possible to write:

```
import { sayHello } from './greeting'
```

But feel free to specify the extension explicitly in case it makes your code more readable.

# Webpack Custom Configuration

So far, we learned that webpack requires us to have an src/index.js file to produce a dist/main.js compiled file. That's the default webpack uses (also called "zero config") as a ready-to-go configuration, but how we can change this if we want to? For example, we would like to change the output file "dist/main.js" to be "build/application.js" instead. Note that we want to change the folder name ("dist" to "build") as well.

## Creating Our Configuration File

With webpack we have the ability to customize a lot of things (including files name and their destination) by using a file called webpack.config.js (that's the name webpack will look for by default). In order to configure itself, you can surely name it something else other than webpack.config.js (for example, "my-config.js" or any other naming you like), but if you do so, just make sure to specify this in the package.json file:

```
scripts: {
  "build": "webpack --config my-config.js"
}
```

Unless you have a reason to do this, the file name webpack.config.js is what webpack will use by default, that's also what most programmers do, so let's keep the default name and create a file called webpack.config.js in the root of our webpack_beginners folder with the following code:

```
module.exports = {
  entry: "./src/index.js",
  output: {
    filename: "main.js"
  }
}
```

Then again, don't forget to run the build command after any change in order to get the desired output:

```
$ npm run build
```

Do you have any idea what will happen? You guessed it … *nothing* different from the previous build! That's because we just wrote what webpack already does for us by default: we specified an entry and ouput file name similar to what a default configuration would be.

## Altering the Default Output

But how can we change the output folder and the output filename to "build/application.js"? The answer is so simple, here is what the new configuration should look like:

```
module.exports = {
  entry: "./src/index.js",
  output: {
    filename: "../build/application.js"
  }
}
```

All we need to do is to replace "main.js" by "../build/application.js". Because the default output folder is "dist," we tell webpack to go back by one step and have our output file "application.js" placed in a new folder called "build." Save and rerun "npm run build" in your terminal, then see the result within your working folder. Figure 2-2 shows the created file.

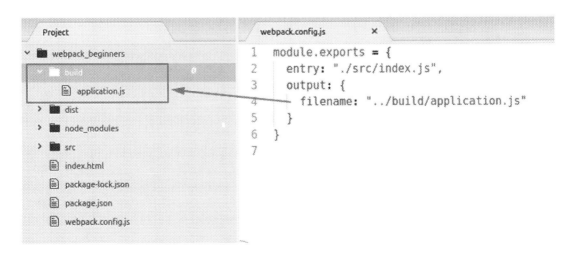

***Figure 2-2.*** *Configuring webpack output folder and file to build/application.js*

While it's possible to write the following in the example above:

```
output: {
  filename: "../build/application.js"
}
```

There is a better way to separate the folder name from the file name by using an option called "path" within our "output" configuration:

```
output: {
  filename: "application.js",
  path: "/home/$USER/path/to/your/build/folder"
}
```

The path should be an absolute path, so make sure to change it where you want your file to be placed, but wait ... writing an absolute path like that is not efficient, as you may want to change your destination folder someday, which implies that you will be obligated to change your configuration file as well every time you do that. Fortunately there is a portable way to do it using a Node JS module called "path."

By installing "path" module and using it in your configuration file, you can get rid of the absolute path and replace it with something dynamic, so first install path module:

```
$ npm install path --save-dev
```

Once the path module is installed, it C be required in webpack.config.js, the best place to require a module is at the top of the file before any code implementation:

```
const path = require('path');
```

Then use it for the "path" option instead of specifying a hard-coded path:

```
path: path.resolve(__dirname, 'build')
```

Listing 2-1 shows the full configuration.

**_Listing 2-1._** Dynamically resolving the working directory using "path" module

```
const path = require('path');
module.exports = {
  entry: "./src/index.js",
  output: {
```

```
    filename: "application.js",
    path: path.resolve(__dirname, 'build')
  }
}
```

Note that we used `path.resolve(__dirname, "build")` instead of our hard-coded absolute path because the "path" module will resolve the directory path for us (where our webpack.config.js is) and then will create a build folder at the same level.

Because we are going to use build/application.js as our output file, you can go ahead and delete the "dist" folder that contains the old "main.js" file, as we won't need it anymore. Also don't forget to update the script tag in your index.html to point to the new "application.js" file. See Listing 2-2.

***Listing 2-2.*** Updating the source of our JavaScript file

```
<!DOCTYPE html>
<html lang="en" dir="ltr">
  <head>
    <meta charset="utf-8">
    <title></title>
  </head>
  <body>
    <script type="text/javascript" src="build/application.js"></script>
  </body>
</html>
```

# Development Mode

In the first chapter, we saw that webpack outputs a warning message in the terminal whenever we try to bundle our JavaScript without specifying the mode option. If you still remember, we addressed that warning by adding --option=production to our webpack command. Basically the production mode will set up our code to be minified as shown in Figure 2-3, which represents the result code of build/application.js after running webpack.

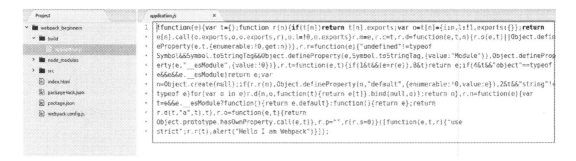

***Figure 2-3.*** *Without "mode" option, the webpack output file is minified by default*

As you might be guessing, the other value that we can use for "mode" option is "development," so let's set "mode" to "development," but this time we prefer to add it to "webpack.config.js" file instead of adding it directly to webpack command. This way we can have all our options in one place; and adding this option is easy like you can see in Listing 2-3.

***Listing 2-3.*** Setting webpack option "mode" to "development"

```
const path = require('path');
module.exports = {
  mode: "development",
  entry: "./src/index.js",
  output: {
    filename: "application.js",
    path: path.resolve(__dirname, 'build')
  }
}
```

By adding the mode option to webpack.config.js, **you should now get rid of the --option=production that we set earlier** in our package.json file. Then, in the terminal, run the bundling command:

```
$ npm run build
```

As result, you can see in Figure 2-4 what happened to our build/application.js file. Our code is no longer minified, and that's what we want to have. When working in development, you can try to switch back to "production" mode and see that the result will be minified like it was before.

**Figure 2-4.** *The outputted code after setting mode to "development"*

If you are curious to see the bundle file produced by webpack, you will find that there is some strange code on there, including some parts that are considered to be "bad practices," such as the famous eval function! I know you might not like this but I'm here to assure you that this won't happen in "production" mode. So during the development phase/mode, webpack doesn't care about quality or performance etc; the goal is to deliver the result and to produce a code that just works!

One last option I would like to mention before moving to the next part is the "watch" option. Whenever we edit our JavaScript, we have to rebuild it in order to get our output file (application.js) updated, and at some point, you will find yourself tired of repeating the command "npm run build" every time a change has been made. But let's face it: as developers, we don't like repetitive tasks, so that's why we automate them all the time. And that's why the option "watch" exists. See Listing 2-4.

**Listing 2-4.** Setting webpack option "watch" to "true"

```
module.exports = {
  watch: true,
  // ...
  // ...
}
```

By setting watch option to true in our webpack.config.js, you will use the command *npm run build* in your terminal one (first) time, and then webpack will update your application.js every time you make a change to one of your source files. Go ahead and try to edit the "alert" we have already put in our "sayHello" function like the following:

```
alert('Hello I am Webpack, am watching you');
```

Go to your browser, refresh, and see. Yes! Webpack is watching your files now, and any update you make is going to be bundled automatically for you.

# Summary

In this chapter, we have seen how to write modules by creating a function in a file and calling it from another one. You can imagine yourself writing more complex code, that needs to be separated in more than 2 or 3 files, so imagine how that can be benefit to you, contrary to writing all your JavaScript in one big file that can be hard to maintain in the long run. We also created a custom configuration file for webpack, and then we changed the output file name and the output destination folder as well. We have set the "mode" option to "development," which unlike the "production" mode results in non-minified code. And finally we used the option "watch" which surveys our code and bundles it whenever a change occurs.

# CHAPTER 3

# Loaders and Plugins

Loaders and plugins are the heart of webpack. They make up the engine that empowers webpack to do the "magical" things for you, like reading and transforming files before passing them to webpack or influencing the output of your bundle by extending the compiler capability, etc. In this chapter, we will be exploring some of the most commonly used loaders and plugins. We will go through examples of how to transpile files from one format to another. We will see how to debug our JavaScript efficiently and how to handle images and optimize them as well as our bundle for fast loading. By the end of this chapter, you will have the necessary understanding of how to use both loaders and plugins in the simplest possible way.

## Loaders vs. Plugins

Loaders, on one hand, tell webpack how to interpret, translate, and make transformations to your source code (for example, from CoffeeScript to vanilla JavaScript, or SASS to CSS). They are like tasks if you are familiar with any other build tool, and basically they preprocess files whenever you import them.

Plugins, on the other hand, can do anything that loaders cannot do. Webpack considers them the backbone of its core. And you will see that they are object-like, they can take arguments, and they can be instantiated as well in order to perform many things or adding functionalities to the compilation such as optimizing your bundle.

In this chapter, we will explore both loaders and plugins, so don't worry too much about the definition. We will get familiar with these two notions when we see the examples. What you have to know, though, is that there are tons of loaders and plugins available (official and third-party ones), and our goal is not to cover them all. Instead we will be focusing on the understanding of how you can apply them and use them in your project, so that in the future if you need to have some additional functionality in your bundling process, you will be able to go and search by yourself, then apply that specific loader or plugin.

© Mohamed Bouzid 2020
M. Bouzid, *Webpack for Beginners*, https://doi.org/10.1007/978-1-4842-5896-5_3

A pattern that you will notice when using loaders and plugins is as follows:

> 1 - installing the loader/plugin (using npm install)
>
> 2 - requiring it (usually we require plugins but not loaders)
>
> 3 - using it (documentation is our valuable friend here)

Again, don't worry if this seems too general for now. Once we start to go through the examples, you will absorb the principle more clearly and get the full picture. So with that in mind, let's start exploring our first loader.

# Using Babel-Loader

Let's assume we want to write ES6 (ECMAScript 6) in our code (which is still not 100% supported yet by all the browsers, especially the old ones, at least at the moment I am writing this). While webpack is able to recognize and translate the "import/export" to its own syntax, it won't do anything for your (other) JavaScript code if you write it in the ES6 style. One of the solutions is to use Babel JS, which is a transpiler that will translate our code from ES6 to ES5.

To use Babel, webpack provides us with a loader called "babel-loader," which is easy and straightforward to use, so let's install it first using our terminal:

```
$ npm install --save-dev babel-loader @babel/core @babel/preset-env
```

If you are wondering how to know what to install exactly in order to get Babel working, the answer is documentation! In order to install any loader or plugin, all you have to do is to search for "Webpack + the name of loader/plugin," then most likely the first link will direct you to the documentation page of that loader or plugin (either webpack website or a GitHub repository) where more details are explained.

Every loader is different in the way it should be used (again, the documentation is how to get details), but the common thing is that they are used as "rules" in the "module" object that we need to add to the webpack configuration file. Listing 3-1 demonstrates an example of babel-loader usage.

***Listing 3-1.*** Configuration of babel-loader in order to transpile ES6 to ES5

```
module.exports = {
  // ...
  output: {
    // ...
```

```
  },
  module: {
    rules: [
      {
        test: /\.m?js$/,
        exclude: /(node_modules|bower_components)/,
        use: {
          loader: 'babel-loader',
          options: {
            presets: ['@babel/preset-env']
          }
        }
      }
    ]
  }
}
```

Note that there is a "module" object, then an array of objects called "rules" where we add the rules for loaders. In this example, we added a rule for Babel; we have basically a "test" key/property with a regular expression "/\.m?js$/" that tells webpack that whenever there is a file with an ".mjs or .js" extension, the babel-loader should be applied to it. The "exclude" property, as its name suggests, tells webpack to skip files if they are node modules or bower components, and then finally the property "use" tells webpack the name of the loader to use, and sets some additional options as well. In this example, the "presets" is set to '@babel/preset-env'.

Do not worry if you are still wondering if you should know somehow about how these things are written or if you should memorize them. Be assured that nobody does. Every loader is different on its own; and your job is to know that you can search a specific loader, copy/past the configuration in your webpack.config.js, and play with it (if needed at all) by exploring the documentation and the available options you can use for that loader.

Now that we have installed babel-loader and we have configured the webpack. config.js file to use it, let's write some ES6 and see if it will work as expected.

In our greeting.js file, using the new ES6 syntax, let's define a variable with the "let" keyword and then use the string interpolation ${} that allows us to put a variable into a string without having the need to concatenate it using the plus (+) sign. Here is our sayHello() function:

```
function sayHello() {
  let tool = 'webpack';
  alert(`Hello I am ${tool}, welcome to ES6`);
}

export { sayHello };
```

Open the terminal and call the webpack/build command:

```
$ npm run build
```

---

**Note**    While we have set the "watch" option to true in the previous chapter to survey our files when updated, in this book I will continue to mention the "*npm run build*" command (for clarity) whenever we make a change to our source files.

---

Go now and take a look at the application.js file, see if the "**let**" keyword was transformed to "**var**," and the interpolation '**Hello I am ${tool}, welcome to ES6**' was transformed to a concatenation. Figure 3-1 shows our application.js file after the translation of our code to ES5.

```
application.js                    ×

95
96    "use strict";
97    eval("__webpack_require__.r(__webpack_exports__);\n/* harmony export (binding) */
 *    __webpack_require__.d(__webpack_exports__, \"sayHello\", function() { return
 *    sayHello; });\nfunction sayHello() {\n  var tool = 'webpack';\n  alert(\"Hello I am
 *    \".concat(tool, \", welcome to ES6\"));\n}\n\n\n//#
 *    sourceURL=webpack:///./src/greeting.js?");
98
99    /***/ }),
100
101   /***/ "./src/index.js":
102   /*!**********************!*\
103     !*** ./src/index.js ***!
104     \**********************/
105   /*! no exports provided */
```

***Figure 3-1.*** *"Let" keyword translated to "var," and the interpolation to "contact" function*

Everything's working fine, our ES6 syntax was transformed to ES5, and so that was it for Babel. Super easy, right? Now you have the tool to use ES6 without worrying about a browser's compatibility; happy coding!

# Debugging Our JavaScript

Let's move on and talk about something I find quite useful when debugging. As we have seen before, webpack wraps our code in modules and injects some extra code in order to make things work in the webpack way. While this does not affect our browsing experience, when we want to debug our code in the browser's developer tools, if there is any error, it will show us application.js (which is the resulting bundled file) as the source of where the error has been triggered instead of the original source code file. That makes debugging hard and sometimes impossible!

## Source Map

The solution? There is a file we can generate called **source map**, which as its name suggests, maps our original source code to the bundled source code generated by webpack, it will be really helpful for us, especially in our development phase.

Webpack provides us with a tool to do this. You can find it under the "Devtool" section on the webpack official website: `https://webpack.js.org/configuration/devtool/`. When you scroll down in the devtool documentation, you will see a table that represents all the possible styles of source mapping you can use. Figure 3-2 is a screenshot taken from the webpack website.

| devtool | build | rebuild | production | quality |
|---|---|---|---|---|
| (none) | fastest | fastest | yes | bundled code |
| eval | fastest | fastest | no | generated code |
| cheap-eval-source-map | fast | faster | no | transformed code (lines only) |
| cheap-module-eval-source-map | slow | faster | no | original source (lines only) |
| eval-source-map | slowest | fast | no | original source |
| cheap-source-map | fast | slow | yes | transformed code (lines only) |
| cheap-module-source-map | slow | slower | yes | original source (lines only) |
| inline-cheap-source-map | fast | slow | no | transformed code (lines only) |
| inline-cheap-module-source-map | slow | slower | no | original source (lines only) |
| source-map | slowest | slowest | yes | original source |
| inline-source-map | slowest | slowest | no | original source |
| hidden-source-map | slowest | slowest | yes | original source |
| nosources-source-map | slowest | slowest | yes | without source content |

***Figure 3-2.*** *Available styles for source mapping*

You may need to choose the one that is the best for you. Here is a little notice about these values from the webpack website:

*Some of these values are suited for development and some for production. For development you typically want fast Source Maps at the cost of bundle size, but for production you want separate Source Maps that are accurate and support minimizing.*

Also note that you can use a plugin to generate the source map, but in our case we are going to just use the "devtool" with **"cheap-module-eval-source-map"** because it's faster when it comes to rebuilding, and because we need it for our development only.

---

**Note**   As mentioned in the webpack documentation, the "cheap-module-eval-source-map" will only show us the line number when debugging, which is enough for our case. But if you think you need other options, then just go ahead and pick whatever is suited for your use case.

---

For revision purposes, Listing 3-2 shows our full webpack.config.js after adding the devtool.

***Listing 3-2.*** Our full webpack.config.js file

```
const path = require('path');
module.exports = {
  watch: true,
  mode: "development",
  devtool: "cheap-module-eval-source-map",
  entry: "./src/index.js",
  output: {
    filename: "application.js",
    path: path.resolve(__dirname, 'build')
  },
  module: {
    rules: [
      {
        test: /\.m?js$/,
        exclude: /(node_modules|bower_components)/,
        use: {
          loader: 'babel-loader',
          options: {
```

```
            presets: ['@babel/preset-env']
          }
        }
      }
    ]
  }
}
```

To understand what devtool can do for us, let's open up the greeting.js file and print something in the browser's console from our `sayHello()` function like it's shown in Listing 3-3.

***Listing 3-3.*** Using console.log to debug in the browser

```
export function sayHello(){
  let tool = 'webpack';
  alert(`Hello I am ${tool}, welcome to ES6`);
  console.log('Can you find me?');
}
```

Save the file and don't forget to re-bundle if you did not do so yet using **npm run build.** Then open the browser console (Ctrl+shift+i or just right-click somewhere in your browser page, choose "Inspect Element" in order to open the developer tool, then navigate to the "console" tab). The console should look like Figure 3-3.

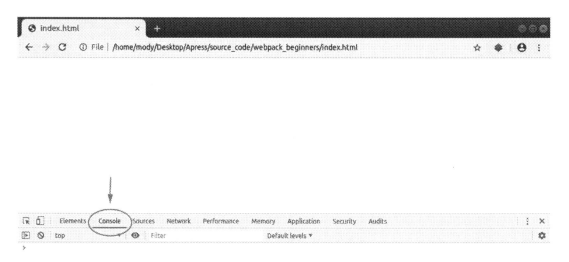

***Figure 3-3.*** *Opening the console in the browser*

Now make sure you open the index.html in the browser (with the console opened) so we can see our message from `sayHello()` function logged (refresh the page if you are not seeing anything yet).

Once the "Can you find me?" message appears in your console, look at the right corner where there is the file name plus the line number that basically tells us exactly where this message comes from and which line specifically. Figure 3-4 shows what I am referring to.

***Figure 3-4.*** *Source map points to the source of our message log*

That's the power of a source map: you can go ahead and click on it to see that it will take you to the right place, meaning the original source file, which is very handy when debugging or when errors appear in our console.

If we haven't used the source map functionality, we would have our console lead us to application.js, which is the bundled file that contains all our JS together, and you may not know which source file the "logged" line is coming from. Now you see the power of a source map and how useful it can be during the development process.

# Handling CSS and SASS Files

As I mentioned earlier, webpack is a bundling tool, not only for JavaScript (which is what it is by default) but also for other types of files as well, including CSS. In this section, we will see how we can bundle CSS and SASS files with webpack.

# Importing CSS in JavaScript

I know what you are probably thinking right now: Why would we import our CSS from a JavaScript file at all? Wouldn't it be better to have the CSS managed separately? Is it a good idea to do that?

Indeed, importing CSS from a JavaScript file is quite useful in many situations. If you are importing a third-party library, for example, a calendar or a date picker that comes with its own styling (CSS files), it makes sense that you load both the JavaScript and CSS of that library at the same place, because it will make it independent from having the code in different locations, which makes the code maintenance a lot easier.

In the following example, I am going to demonstrate how you can load CSS from a JavaScript file, but we won't use a third-party library. Instead we will just simulate that by creating a CSS file within our source code folder and load it in our index.js file. Let's create a file and name it "lib.css" in our "src" folder, and let's write the following rule in it to change the background color of our page:

```
body{
  background-color: magenta;
}
```

We will then import that CSS file in our index.js (at the top) file using:

```
import lib from './lib.css';
```

After that, we will need to bundle our JS, so from our terminal using:

```
$ npm run build
```

Oops! We have gotten an error saying that *"You may need an appropriate loader to handle this file type, currently no loaders are configured to process this file ..."* Figure 3-5 is a screenshot taken from my terminal showing the error message I'm talking about.

**Figure 3-5.**  *Webpack failed to process our css file*

The error in Figure 3-5 shows up because webpack doesn't recognize our CSS file. Webpack knows only how to deal with JavaScript, but if you need to import anything other than JavaScript, you have to configure webpack in order to be able to use it.

## Loading CSS with CSS-Loader

As we have seen before with babel-loader, any file that will be detected as a ".js" file will be transpiled from ES6 to ES5. For the CSS we are going to use exactly the same technique, detecting any file with a ".css" extension and make it recognizable for webpack. That's why we need a loader called "css-loader," which we are going to use in the next step.

First install css-loader with our terminal:

```
$ npm install css-loader --save-dev
```

When the installation is finished, add the CSS rule to your webpack.config.js "rules" like Listing 3-4 shows.

***Listing 3-4.*** Adding "css-loader" to rules for webpack to handle css file

```
const path = require('path');
module.exports = {
  // ...
  module: {
    rules: [
      {
        test: /\.m?js$/,
        // ...
      },
      {
        test: /\.css$/i,
        use: ['css-loader'],
      }
    ]
  }
}
```

Again, if you are wondering where I came from with these configuration lines, just search for "webpack css-loader," and you will get the link to the webpack documentation page that explains it. Finally, let's bundle our files using the command:

```
$ npm run build
```

See that the error we had before disappeared, and webpack is now able to load CSS files. But that's not all. We still need to make our imported CSS applied to the index.html page, so we are going to use another loader called "style-loader."

# Injecting CSS to Our HTML

What "style-loader" will do for us, is take the imported CSS in the index.js file and inject it into the DOM between <style></style> tags.

Again, you will need to install it first:

```
$ npm install style-loader --save-dev
```

Then add it to the previous css-loader rule we added above (refer back to Listing 3-4), so the rule will become:

```
{
  test: /\.css$/i,
  use: ['style-loader', 'css-loader'],
}
```

Note here that we are using two loaders for files that have a ".css" extension. Also note that the **order** we put in these loaders is **important.** You might be guessing that the first loader at the left (style-loader) will be applied first, then the second one (css-loader) will be applied after it. But the reality is that the order webpack will use is the opposite: the order starts from the right to the left:

> 1- Webpack will use "css-loader" (that will transform our CSS into CommonJS)
>
> 2- The "style-loader" will be used secondly (which will inject that CSS in our page <head>)

Now let's bundle our files:

```
$ npm run build
```

Then open index.html file in the browser, and see that the magenta is applied.

If we inspect using the browser console, we will see that a <style> tag was injected dynamically to our page by JavaScript, with the styling we imported from lib.css file. See Figure 3-6.

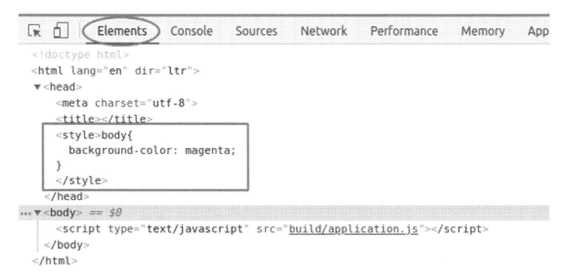

*Figure 3-6.* *CSS injected to our HTML file by webpack*

But what if you would like to use some preprocessor like SASS? Well, in order to recognize SASS, webpack will need two loaders, which we will be exploring next.

# Compiling SASS to CSS

In order for webpack to be able to load SASS files, we need a loader called "sass-loader" and another one for the compilation called "node-sass." Let's try this and install both of these loaders from our terminal.

```
$ npm install sass-loader node-sass --save-dev
```

After the installation completes, we need to add another rule to the webpack.config.js like this:

```
{
  test: /\.scss$/i,
  use: ['style-loader', 'css-loader', 'sass-loader'],
}
```

Here we are testing if the file ends with ".scss" If so, we apply the "sass-loader" to it first. After that, "sass-loader" recognizes and compiles our SASS files, the "css-loader" will read that CSS turns it to CommonJS, and then our "style-loader" will inject it in the DOM dynamically via JavaScript.

**Note**    Remember that the order of applying loaders is from right to left), so the "sass-loader" will be used first, which itself calls "node-sass" to compile SASS to CSS (without requiring us to call it explicitly).

To test if this is working, go ahead and create a SASS file under the "src" folder, name it "application.scss," and then let's write some SASS syntax into it:

```
$gradient: linear-gradient(to right, #00467f, #a5cc82);
body{
  background-image: $gradient;
}
```

DO NOT FORGET to import application.scss in the index.js file:

```
import application from "./application.scss"
```

Save the file, then in the terminal use the command:

```
$ npm run build
```

Open index.html file in the browser and see that the background gradient was applied to our page. Also, if you check the console, you will notice, as shown in Figure 3-7, that another <style> tag was added to the head of the page containing the (compiled) styles we have in our application.scss file.

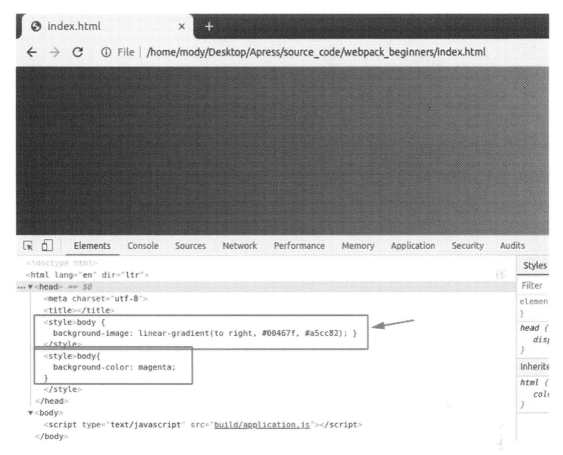

***Figure 3-7.*** *Webpack is now recognizing scss files and the gradient color is applied*

Now that we are able to use CSS and SASS in our project, let's talk about browser compatibility and how we can apply vendor prefixes to our CSS using postcss-loader.

# Prefixing CSS with Vendor Prefixes

Not all CSS features are fully supported by all browsers, so that's why we need to use browser prefixes or what we call vendor prefixes. An example of this case is the linear-gradient color we used previously, and which can be prefixed as follows:

```
background: -webkit-gradient(linear, left top, right top, from(#00467f),
to(#a5cc82));
background: -o-linear-gradient(left, #00467f, #a5cc82);
background: linear-gradient(to right, #00467f, #a5cc82)
```

Using "postcss-loader" will allow us to do that automatically and add all the necessary prefixes without having to specify them ourselves, which is super cool. Let's install it from our terminal:

```
$ npm install postcss-loader --save-dev
```

Here is a link to the documentation where the "postcss-loader" is documented: https://webpack.js.org/loaders/postcss-loader/. If you scroll down, you will find a recommended way to use it in the webpack.config.js file. Listing 3-5 shows what our CSS and SCSS rules will become after applying "postcss-loader."

***Listing 3-5.*** Applying css-loader to our css/scss files

```
{
  test: /\.css$/i,
  use: ['style-loader', 'css-loader', 'postcss-loader'],
},
{
  test: /\.scss$/i,
  use: ['style-loader', 'css-loader', 'postcss-loader', 'sass-loader'],
}
```

If you read the documentation carefully, there is an important note saying:

> *This loader cannot be used with CSS Modules out of the box due to the way css-loader processes file imports. To make them work properly, either add the css-loader's importLoaders option, or use postcss-modules instead of css-loader.*

In our case, we are going to use the option `importLoaders` to prevent any issue with css-loader. Listing 3-6 shows the updated snippet.

***Listing 3-6.*** Using importLoaders option to prevent issues with css-loader

```
{
  test: /\.css$/i,
  use: [
    'style-loader',
    { loader: 'css-loader', options: { importLoaders: 1 } },
```

```
      'postcss-loader'
    ],
  },
  {
    test: /\.scss$/i,
    use: [
      'style-loader',
      { loader: 'css-loader', options: { importLoaders: 1 } },
      'postcss-loader',
      'sass-loader'
    ],
  }
```

All we did here is replace the string 'css-loader' by an object where we specify the name of the loader, and we set additional options. In this case, we have set importLoaders to 1.

Another thing we need to do in order to make "postcss-loader" work like we want is to use a plugin called "autoprefixer." We have to alter our previous code slightly and change 'postcss-loader' from a string to an object where we can add some more options like specifying which browsers we should add prefixes to.

---

**Note**    You can specify these browsers using `browserlist` property in the package.json file. But as we want to keep this option in our config file for this example, I am going to use another property called `overrideBrowserslist` that will work fine too.

---

Here is what our 'postcss-loader' string should become:

```
{
  loader: 'postcss-loader',
  options: {
    plugins: [
      require('autoprefixer')({
      overrideBrowserslist: ['last 3 versions', 'ie >9']
      })
    ]
  }
}
```

Listing 3-7 shows the rules for both CSS and SCSS.

***Listing 3-7.*** Full rules for CSS and SCSS files

```
const path = require('path');
module.exports = {
  // ...
  module: {
    rules: [
      // ...
      {
        test: /\.css$/i,
        use: [
          'style-loader',
          { loader: 'css-loader', options: { importLoaders: 1 } },
          {
            loader: 'postcss-loader',
            options: {
              plugins: [
                require('autoprefixer')({
                overrideBrowserslist: ['last 3 versions', 'ie >9']
                })
              ]
            }
          }
        ],
      },
      {
        test: /\.scss$/i,
        use: [
          'style-loader',
          { loader: 'css-loader', options: { importLoaders: 1 } },
          {
            loader: 'postcss-loader',
            options: {
              plugins: [
                require('autoprefixer')({
```

```
                overrideBrowserslist: ['last 3 versions', 'ie >9']
              })
          ]
        }
      },
      'sass-loader'
    ],
  }
  ]
  }
}
```

Don't forget to **install "autoprefixer"** before proceeding:

$ npm install autoprefixer --save-dev

Then run webpack to get our bundle updated:

$ npm run build

If you remember, we were using "linear-gradient" in the application.scss file. Now, if you open the file index.html in the browser and you see the styles injected in the page (from the web console), you will see that gradient was autoprefixed with the necessary prefixes like those shown in Figure 3-8.

***Figure 3-8.*** *Vendor prefixes applied to "linear-gradient" by autoprefixer*

In this case, two prefixes were added, one for webkit browsers and another one for opera. This can be really useful when dealing with CSS and can save you a considerable amount of time and effort.

# Extract CSS to Its Own Separate File

Now that we have configured what we need for our CSS/SCSS to work, there is one thing though that is kind of annoying: our CSS is injected in the index.html page between <style></style> tags. That might be okay when we have just some few styles, but if we have a lot of CSS, then embedding it directly within our HTML page is not a good idea at all.

With webpack, we can extract the CSS we imported to its own file with the help of a plugin called "mini-css-extract-plugin." Let's try to do it by first installing it:

```
$ npm install --save-dev mini-css-extract-plugin
```

Once the plugin installed, this time you have to require it at the top of webpack config file (webpack.config.js):

```
const MiniCssExtractPlugin = require("mini-css-extract-plugin");
```

To use the plugin, just add the following to the configuration object:

```
plugins: [
  new MiniCssExtractPlugin({
    filename: 'application.css'
  })
]
```

Here, we created a "plugins" property that takes a hash (of plugins) as value; we instantiated our MiniCssExtractPlugin and we passed a filename (application.css) to it as an argument.

Wait, that's not all. We still have the "style-loader" doing the job of injecting CSS into our HTML page. We need to change it from using "style-loader" here:

```
{
  test: /\.css$/i,
  use: [
```

```
    'style-loader',
     // ...
  ]
}
```

To use `MiniCssExtractPlugin.loader` instead:

```
{
  test: /\.css$/i,
  use: [
    MiniCssExtractPlugin.loader,
    // ...
  ]
}
```

The same thing applies to our SCSS files:

```
{
  test: /\.scss$/i,
  use: [
    'style-loader',
    // ...
  ]
}
```

Which should become:

```
{
  test: /\.scss$/i,
  use: [
    MiniCssExtractPlugin.loader,
    // ...
  ]
}
```

Now back to the terminal. Use the command *"npm run build"* to bundle our files, and let's see if this time we will have our CSS extracted in a separate file, Figure 3-9 confirms that it does.

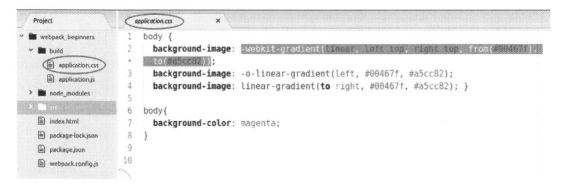

**Figure 3-9.** *Extracting our styles to a separate application.css file*

If you check your build folder, you will find a new created file "application.css" that contains all our CSS from "lib.css" and "application.scss." But now if you open the index. html in your browser, the styles are gone. That's normal because we are no longer using "style-loader" so our styles are no longer injected in the HTML page. We need to specify a link to our stylesheet between <head></head> of the index.html file, as the following:

```
<link rel="stylesheet" href="build/application.css">
```

Go to your browser and see that our page styling are back. Very cool!

Note that our CSS is not minified because we are using "development" mode; if we change that to "production," it will be minified, right? Let's try and change mode to "production" in our webpack.config.js as follows:

```
module.exports = {
  mode: "production",
  // ...
  // ...
}
```

Don't forget to run the command "***npm run build***" to bundle. Then, go to the build folder. You'll see that our application.js is minified, but our application.css is not. Webpack will do the minification *only* for JavaScript files; anything else, you need to add it and specify it by yourself.

# Minifying the Extracted CSS

So how are we going to minify a CSS file? There is another plugin that we can use called "optimize-css-assets-webpack-plugin," which will help us do exactly this. First, install the plugin:

```
$ npm install optimize-css-assets-webpack-plugin --save-dev
```

Then we need to require it at the top of our webpack.config.js:

```
const OptimizeCSSAssetsPlugin = require('optimize-css-assets-webpack-plugin');
```

Webpack documentation suggests using the "optimization.minimizer" setting, seen as follows:

```
optimization: {
  minimizer: [
    new TerserJSPlugin({}),
    new OptimizeCSSAssetsPlugin({})
  ],
}
```

Note that besides the "OptimizeCSSAssetsPlugin," there is another one called "TerserJSPlugin," which is a plugin that already comes with webpack. You won't need to install it yourself; that's the plugin used by default to minify your JavaScript when you use "production" mode. However, the thing you need to do is require it at the top of your webpack configuration file:

```
const TerserJSPlugin = require('terser-webpack-plugin');
```

You may ask why we are using TerserJSPlugin explicitly above when we know it's already used by default to minify our JavaScript?

Well, as it is stated in the webpack documentation:

> *Setting optimization.minimizer overrides the defaults provided by web-pack, so make sure to also specify a JS minimizer.*

This means that by using optimization.minimizer in your webpack.config.js, it will override the default behavior of webpack (for minimization) so you need to specify explicitly all the plugins you need to use for the minification part. Listing 3-8 shows what webpack.config.js should look like after requiring the necessary plugins and the usage of optimization.minimizer.

***Listing 3-8.*** Usage of the plugins needed to minify both JavaScript and CSS

```
const path = require('path');
const MiniCssExtractPlugin = require("mini-css-extract-plugin");
const OptimizeCSSAssetsPlugin = require('optimize-css-assets-webpack-
plugin');
const TerserJSPlugin = require('terser-webpack-plugin');

module.exports = {
  watch: true,
  mode: "production",
  devtool: "cheap-module-eval-source-map",
  entry: "./src/index.js",
  output: {
    filename: "application.js",
    path: path.resolve(__dirname, 'build')
  },
  optimization: {
    minimizer: [
      new TerserJSPlugin({}),
      new OptimizeCSSAssetsPlugin({})
    ],
  },
  module: {
    // ...
  },
  plugins: [
    // ...
  ]
}
```

Now you can run the bundle command in your terminal:

```
$ npm run build
```

Take a look at the build folder files (application.js and application.css). You will find that the code of both files is minified as expected.

# Handling Images

One last thing I want to discuss before moving into the next chapter is using images in your CSS. For example, in case you are using the "background-image" property with an image as value, webpack won't be able to recognize it. But, like other types of files, there are loaders that will make this possible, so in this section we will discuss how we can handle images with webpack.

# Loading Image Files

I am going to use an image of a cat here from pixabay (which is a website full of free images), but you can grab any image you want. If you prefer to use the image I'm using, please refer to the source files accompanying this book.

Once you have the image in your computer, rename it to cat.jpg (for clarity) and then put it into the "src" folder.

Let's change our page background, by replacing the contents of the "application.scss" file as follows:

```
body{
  background-image: url('cat.jpg');
  background-size: cover;
}
```

The background-size property here is just to make sure the background image expands to the full width and height of our screen, so it will look better. Go back to your terminal and run webpack using:

```
$ npm run build
```

As you might be expecting, webpack throws an error because we have no loader yet to process images, so you should get a long red message saying, "*You may need an appropriate loader to handle this file type, currently no loaders are configured to process this file.*"

In order to recognize images, webpack will need two loaders: one called "url-loader" and another one called "file-loader." What these loaders do is basically the same, but "url-loader" will serve us a lot when dealing with small images or icons; it will directly transform any small image to base64 code and insert it for us instead of url('...'). That will help reduce the call to the server for every small icon or image set in our CSS. Let's start first by installing "url-loader" and go from there:

```
$ npm install url-loader --save-dev
```

In our webpack.config.js, we will add another rule that checks for files ending with extensions related to images (jpg, gif, png, etc). Here is the rule that I am going to add:

```
{
  test: /\.(png|jpg|gif|svg)$/i,
  use: [
    {
      loader: 'url-loader',
      options: {
        limit: 8192,
      },
    },
  ],
}
```

Again, for the usage of any plugin or loader, you have to check the webpack documentation or its GitHub page. For "url-loader," here is the direct link to the documentation: `https://webpack.js.org/loaders/url-loader/`.

Here, we are using the "url-loader" with a "limit" option. What this option does is; for all our images with a size less or equal 8192 (size <= 8192) bytes, it encodes them as base64 and injects the result into our CSS instead of url('...'). Let's open the terminal and see what will happen by calling the build command:

```
$  npm run build
```

What you will get is a different error. Webpack was able to recognize our image but finds that our image is more than the limit we specified (8192). If you read the thrown error, it says, "***Cannot find module 'file-loader,***" which means we had to use another loader called "file-loader." Let's go ahead and get it installed:

```
$ npm install file-loader --save-dev
```

Don't run the command "***npm run build***" just yet, because we still need to specify a "name" option within the "url-loader" rule.

So far, we used the "limit" option, which can be of three types: Number|Boolean|String. In our case, we used a Number (that represents the max size of a file in bytes). If you check the documentation of "url-loader," there is a part that says:

*If the file size is equal or greater than the limit file-loader will be used (by default) and all query parameters are passed to it.*

What this means is, that "url-loader" will try to turn our images to base64 (based on a size limit) but if the file has equal or greater size than what we specify, the "file-loader" will be used instead, and if any parameter there (for the "url-loader") it will be passed to the "file-loader.". In our case, we are going to add the "name" option to our "url-loader" so if the file is equal or greater than the limit size, that option will be used for the loaded file:

```
{
  test: /\.(png|jpg|gif|svg)$/i,
  use: [
    {
      loader: 'url-loader',
      options: {
        limit: 8192,
        name: '[name].[hash:7].[ext]'
      },
    },
  ],
}
```

Note that we used a template: '[name].[hash:7].[ext]'. We will discuss what this is in the next chapter, but all you have to know for now is that the "url-loader" will take our file and save it (thanks to the file-loader) to the build folder by giving it a name composed of the original file name followed by a hash, followed by the original file's extension and each part separated by a dot. So, in our case, given the template we specified above, "cat.jpg" will become something like "cat.1c28f43.jpg".

Note that the hash "1c28f43" was resulted from the hash algorithm used by webpack based on the content of the file, so you'll get a different hash whenever the image file changed.

Now it's time to re-bundle our source files using the command:

```
$ npm run build
```

If you did everything correctly, you will see no errors. But what just happened?

Check the "build" folder and see that our image was saved there, and the best part is that webpack has outputted that name dynamically for us in our generated "application. css" file. Here is what I've gotten in my CSS:

```
body{background-image:url(cat.1c28f43.jpg);background-
size:cover;background-color:#f0f}
```

Let's make sure it's working by opening the index.html file in the browser, Figure 3-10 shows our page with the cat background image.

***Figure 3-10.** Cat image applied to the page background*

---

**Note**    If you don't want the possibility to turn your "small-sized" images to inline base64 images, you can use "file-loader" directly instead of "url-loader," and that would be fine too.

---

That's all for this part, in the next step, we will see how we can reduce the size of our image in order to make it load fast by using Webpack Image Loader.

# Compressing Images

Before we compress our image, I would like to show you my terminal screenshot (from the last build) which demonstrates the size of the bundled files. The cat image in Figure 3-11 has the size of 20.5 KiB.

```
Built at: 01/05/2020 4:12:37 PM
            Asset     Size  Chunks           Chunk Name
application.css  87 bytes       0  [emitted]  main
 application.js  3.07 KiB       0  [emitted]  main
cat.1c28f43.jpg  20.5 KiB          [emitted]
Entrypoint main = application.css application.js
[0] ./src/application.scss 39 bytes {0} [built]
[1] ./src/lib.css 39 bytes {0} [built]
```

***Figure 3-11.*** *The size of bundled files after compilation*

Webpack has a loader called **Image-Webpack-Loader** that can be used to compress PNG, JPEG, GIF, SVG and WEBP images. From its GitHub repository, as a note for macOS users, when installing this loader, it may complain about missing "libpng" dependency. In this case, if you are a Mac user, then you may need to install that library first using the command:

```
$ brew install libpng
```

To install the loader:

```
$ npm install image-webpack-loader --save-dev
```

Now let's use the "image-webpack-loader" in our webpack config file. All we need to do is add another loader for our images:

```
{
  test: /\.(png|jpg|gif|svg)$/i,
  use: [
    {
      loader: 'url-loader',
      options: {
        limit: 8192,
        name: '[name].[hash:7].[ext]'
      },
```

```
    },
    { loader: 'image-webpack-loader' }
  ],
}
```

Then run the build command from the terminal:

$ npm run build

Finally, let's check the image size again. Figure 3-12 shows the new size of the image after using the ImageWebpackPlugin.

```
ᴅuᴛᴛᴛ ᴀᴛ: 01/05/2020 4:25:05 ᴘᴍ
                Asset        Size    Chunks              Chunk Name
application.css    87 bytes        0  [emitted]   main
 application.js    3.07 KiB        0  [emitted]   main
cat.7050c9c.jpg    12.5 KiB           [emitted]
Entrypoint main = application.css application.js
[0] ./src/application.scss 39 bytes {0} [built]
[1] ./src/lib.css 39 bytes {0} [built]
```

***Figure 3-12.***  *The new image size after applying ImageWebpackPlugin*

See that our cat image size has decreased from 20.5 KiB to 12.5 KiB, which is super cool. Imagine what that can do for you when you have bigger images; it's a very useful loader that I recommend using whenever possible when loading images.

There is one last note about the regular expression we used for our "file-loader" which is currently limited to image files (/\.(png|jpg|gif|svg)$/i). You may want to add more file formats, like fonts for example. Here is an extended RegEx that you can use for this purpose:

/(png|jpg|gif|svg|woff2?|eot|ttf|otf|wav)(\?.*)?$/i

Here, we just added some file extensions like woff2, eot, ttf etc, that it's possible to load with the file-loader, but you can basically add any other type of file, loaders are here for that purpose. At this point, you start to see the power of webpack, and how you can configure it to do a lot of helpful things for you. Once you grasp the syntax, you can even separate your configuration file to multiple files and include them as part of the main webpack.config.js if this later gets bigger (or in case you find it hard to read), but for the sake of simplicity in this book, we will stick with one file only.

# Summary

This was a long chapter about loaders and plugins, but I wanted to provide you with as many examples as possible in order for you to understand the concept and to see the difference between both. We have seen how to use Babel in order to write modern JavaScript, and we have explored source mapping, which allows us to debug our code efficiently. We have also seen how to use CSS and SASS loaders to recognize and bundle our stylesheets, as well as images, without forgetting the minimization of our assets and the optimization of our images. The possibilities are endless with webpack as you can imagine; there are a lot of loaders and plugins out there that can do all kinds of things you may think of. At this point, I hope you are ready to explore more loaders and plugins on your own and use them in your future projects. With that said, it's time to move on to a new chapter.

# CHAPTER 4

# Cache

This chapter is mainly about dealing with caches and how we can automate the process of naming our files in a way that will ensure the browser fetches the latest version of resources when those resources are updated. We will see how to use substitutions, which are nothing more than placeholders for strings resolved at compilation time, in order to compose the names of our files and also to add the necessary hash string to it. Finally, we will see how to update those file names in our HTML dynamically whenever an asset is updated.

## Output Files Naming

So far, we have used webpack to build one JavaScript file (application.js) that contains all our JavaScript, but there are many cases where you may want to have multiple files, and maybe you want to use each one on different pages of your web application.

Let's, for example, assume you want to create one file "application.js" for your main app or global website and another one called "admin.js" for your admin area. How would you produce two separated files in this case?

First, in your "src" folder, create another file and name it "admin.js". Let's write a dummy function on how that would look:

```
function welcome(){
  alert('Welcome to the admin area');
}
```

In our webpack.config.js, if you remember the "entry" option we have, it looks like this:

```
entry: "./src/index.js"
```

© Mohamed Bouzid 2020
M. Bouzid, *Webpack for Beginners*, https://doi.org/10.1007/978-1-4842-5896-5_4

Webpack allows us to set more than one entry, by specifying an object where each property name will serve us later for composing output file names, and the value is the relative path to the source file for that entry.

Go ahead and try this by changing the "entry" option in your webpack.config.js as follows:

```
entry: {
  application: "./src/index.js",
  admin: "./src/admin.js"
}
```

The next step is to tell webpack to use the property names (application and admin) we have in our "entry" object (remember that these property names will serve us for composing the names of our generated files). Currently the "output" option is as follows:

```
output: {
  filename: "application.js",
  path: path.resolve(__dirname, 'build')
}
```

You notice that currently the generated filename is called "application.js." In order to use the "entry" property names as the names for the output files, we need to replace the hard-coded "application.js" by something dynamic, what I refer to here is a substitution called [name]. Basically what you need to do is to replace "application" by the placeholder [name] like this:

```
output: {
  filename: "[name].js",
  path: path.resolve(__dirname, 'build')
}
```

Webpack will use the "entry" property names and create your output files based on those names. If you bundle now using "***npm run build***," you will see that your build folder will contain two JavaScript files: "application.js" and "admin.js" as shown in Figure 4-1.

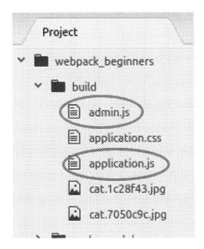

***Figure 4-1.*** *The configured entry property names "admin" and "application" turned to JS files with same name due to the [name] substitution specified in the output setting*

Equally, we can do the same for our CSS. So far, we have the "MiniCssExtractPlugin" in our configuration file extracting the CSS to a file called "application.css" as follows:

```
plugins: [
  new MiniCssExtractPlugin({
    filename: "application.css"
  })
]
```

If you remember, the "index.js" file has the following lines at the top:

```
import application from "./application.scss"
import lib from "./lib.css"
// ...
```

That's fine as far as we have our CSS imported from that file only. Let's try to move the line containing the importation of "lib.css" from index.js to the first line of "admin.js" and then run:

```
$ npm run build
```

Take a look at your terminal and see what happened. As shown in Figure 4-2, there is an error about a conflict that resulted from multiple chunks trying to emit assets to the same file name, application.css.

```
ERROR in chunk application [entry]
application.css
Conflict: Multiple chunks emit assets to the same filename applicat
ion.css (chunks 0 and 1)
```

**Figure 4-2.** *Error while bundling because of multiple chunks trying to be bundled in one CSS file*

What this error is basically saying is that we are importing CSS in more than one JavaScript file and outputting them in one CSS file, and that's why we need to use the same technique we used with our JS files, which is [name] placeholder. All you need to do is replace "application.css" in the MiniCssExtractPlugin filename option by [name]. css as follows:

```
plugins: [
  new MiniCssExtractPlugin({
    filename: "[name].css"
  })
]
```

Let's check again by calling webpack:

```
$ npm run build
```

Now if you check the "build" folder, you will see a new generated css file called "admin.css". Since we imported "lib.css" in "admin.js," you see that it was extracted to a separate "admin.css" file, while the "application.scss" we imported in "application.js" was extracted to "application.css" file. The output files are shown in Figure 4-3.

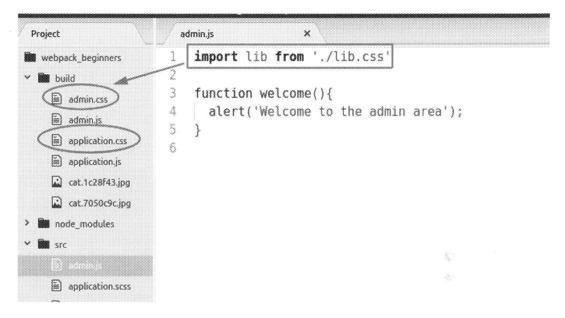

***Figure 4-3.*** *A separate admin.css created after importing "lib.css" in admin.js*

If you are wondering why the output CSS file name is "admin.css" and not "lib.css," that's because the [name] substitution is based on the entry's property name corresponding to the file where that CSS was imported. That means for both our entry properties here:

```
entry: {
  application: "./src/index.js",
  admin: "./src/admin.js"
}
```

We have an equivalent CSS file whose name corresponds to each one of the property names ("application" and "admin") so all our imported CSS in application.js will be in application.css, and all our imported CSS in admin.js will be in admin.css.

Now that we have seen the notion of "substitution," let's talk about something really useful when it comes to our assets in production: cache busting.

# Adding Hash Content

Any node on the network (such as reverse proxy caches, CDNs, gateway caches, web proxy caches, etc.) between the origin server up to and including your browser can potentially cache resources to reduce server load, network traffic, and latency.

Resources that change infrequently like JavaScript and CSS files are among those that can potentially benefit the most.

For instance, the origin web server can be configured to send a header telling caches to save a copy of those resources for one year. That's a whole year of resources being served by a web browser's private cache or intermediate shared caches and not going all the way to the origin server.

But what happens if you need to fix a bug in your JavaScript code or need to update the layout of your webpage through the CSS file **before** they have expired?

To solve this issue, web developers have come up with a technique for circumventing the cache (a.k.a. cache busting), which consists of adding a unique resource version identifier in such a way that the browser asks for a new resource, instead of the old cached one.

There are basically three methods for resource name versioning:

- File name versioning (example: application-ers4e54aem1v8e.js)

- File path versioning (example: /v3/application.js)

- Query string versioning (application.js?version=3)

We will focus here on filename versioning. This is what most websites do to bust caches; we can use it simply by adding a hash string to the name of our file.

Webpack has a substitution for that named [contenthash] that can be used in your configuration file. Let's first add it to our output:

```
output: {
  filename: "[name]-[contenthash].js",
  path: path.resolve(__dirname, 'build')
}
```

Then to our MiniCssExtractPlugin as well:

```
plugins: [
  new MiniCssExtractPlugin({
    filename: "[name]-[contenthash].css"
  })
]
```

Note that we have used a dash character (-) between the substitutions for name and content hash. You will find many developers using a dot (.) instead; that's fine too – use whatever you like.

There are many other placeholders or substitutions that you can use besides [name] and [contenthash] that are shown in Figure 4-4.

| Template | Description |
| --- | --- |
| [hash] | The hash of the module identifier |
| [contenthash] | the hash of the content of a file, which is different for each asset |
| [chunkhash] | The hash of the chunk content |
| [name] | The module name |
| [id] | The module identifier |
| [query] | The module query, i.e., the string following ? in the filename |
| [function] | The function, which can return filename [ string ] |

*Figure 4-4.* *Available hash substitutions for caching. Source:* `https://v4.webpack.js.org/configuration/output/#outputfilename`

Note that substitutions may have different meanings to different parts of webpack such as loaders or plugins.

For instance, back in Chapter 3, we used the substitution [hash:7] in the configuration for url-loader. In that loader, hash and contenthash are both based on calculations over the contents of the file.

It's time to use our terminal and re-bundle using `npm run build`. Let's see what we will get this time. Figure 4-5 shows the generated files after adding the contenthash substitution.

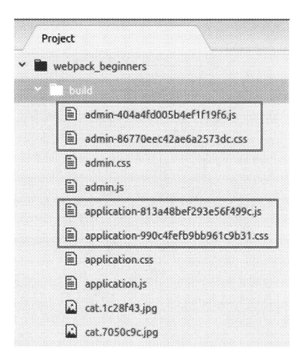

***Figure 4-5.*** *The contenthash added to our JavaScript and CSS files*

As you see, webpack created our JavaScript and CSS files but with a content hash appended to the name of each file. Your content hash might be different than mine, but the idea here is to have that hash in the file name to circumvent caches when the resource gets updated.

What will happen next is if you add or change the code in one of your files, webpack will generate a file with a different content hash. As an example, we will open our admin. js file (in the "src" folder) and add some code to it. Let's add another function like the following:

```
function calculate(a, b){
  console.log(a+b);
}
```

Use the command "***npm run build***" to bundle our files. Then see what will happen inside our build folder as shown in Figure 4-6.

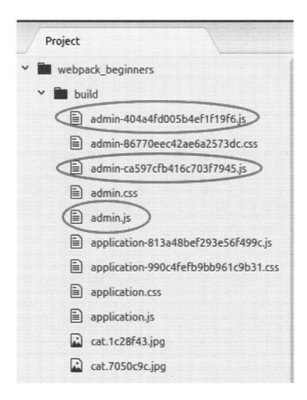

***Figure 4-6.*** *Multiple versions of the admin\*.js file. The first one still without a hash and the following two revisions*

In addition to the original admin.js file (we got before we started using [contenthash] placeholder) and the other admin-*.js that has a contenthash, webpack just created a third admin-*.js file with a different contenthash, and that's because the content of our src/admin.js file has changed for the second time.

Webpack creates a file name containing a new hash every time the content of a file gets updated in order to bust the caching of the old file by telling caches it should fetch the new updated file and cache that instead. The same applies to CSS files.

# Cleaning the Build Directory

Like we have seen, whenever something changes in one of our source files, webpack will create a new file of it with a different contenthash without deleting the old one. For example, in the case of admin.js we have three variations:

- admin.js

- admin-**First-Generated-Hash-Substitution**.js

- admin-**Second-Generated-Hash-Substitution** .js

What we want to have instead is a single version of the bundled file every time the contents changed. There is a way to do this using a plugin called "clean-webpack-plugin," which is a plugin that will clean our build folder every time we generate a new build. This way, you will only have the latest generated files. As you may have guessed, we have to install it first before using it:

```
$ npm install --save-dev clean-webpack-plugin
```

Once done, as we used to do with plugins, we need to require it in the webpack.config.js file:

```
const { CleanWebpackPlugin } = require('clean-webpack-plugin');
```

Note that I used curly braces {} around the variable name. That is called object destructuring and the assignment is equivalent to:

```
const CleanWebpackPlugin = require('clean-webpack-plugin').
CleanWebpackPlugin;
```

This is needed because of how the module authors chose to export the object within the module.

Now let's go ahead and use it in the plugin section of webpack config file:

```
plugins: [
  new CleanWebpackPlugin(),
  new MiniCssExtractPlugin({
    filename: '[name]-[contenthash].css'
  })
]
```

It's time to run the webpack command in our terminal and see if our "build" folder will be cleaned when webpack outputs the result of our bundling:

```
$ npm run build
```

Take a look at our build folder and see that there is only one variant of each bundled file. Figure 4-7 below shows the resulting files we will get.

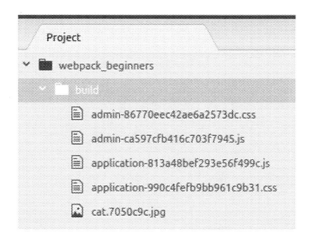

***Figure 4-7.*** *Our "build" folder cleaned after using CleanWebpackPlugin*

Everything looks fine so far, but let's think a bit about our "index.html" file. I'm talking about the following lines:

```
<link rel="stylesheet" href="build/application.css">
<script type="text/JavaScript" src="build/application.js"></script>
```

I know, we should maybe add a link to admin.css and admin.js as well, but this is not what I want to draw your attention to. What I'm trying to explain is that we will need to add the name (plus the content hash) of our JavaScript and CSS files, and update them every time the hash content changes for that file, but who wants to do a repetitive task like this? Let's jump in to the next section and see if we can do it in a more efficient way.

# Manifest Plugin

As we mentioned before, every time the content hash of our JavaScript or CSS files change, we need to go and update our index.html to point to the right file, but we want a more automatic way to do it. We will see one way of doing it with a plugin called "webpack-manifest-plugin," but we won't go deep into the usage inside our HTML (all we need to understand is the main idea). Then in the next section, we will see an alternative way. For now, let's install our plugin:

```
$ npm install --save-dev webpack-manifest-plugin
```

Then require it in the webpack.config.js:

```
const WebpackManifestPlugin = require('webpack-manifest-plugin');
```

Finally use it by adding an instance of WebpackManifestPlugin to the array of your plugins:

```
plugins: [
  new WebpackManifestPlugin(),
  // ...
]
```

Once it's done, go to your terminal and run the build command, then see what happened.

```
$ npm run build
```

A new JSON file called "manifest.json" was added to our "build" folder like you see in Figure 4-8.

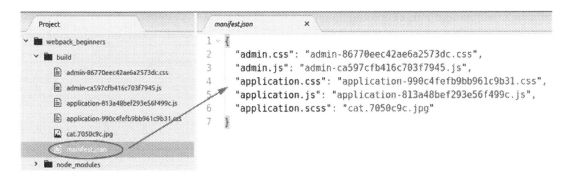

***Figure 4-8.*** *A "manifest.json" file generated that contains every file name with a simplified key*

What you can do now with that file is to access it dynamically using a server-side language (like PHP or Ruby or Node, etc.). Then, instead of hard-coding the name of the static files (JS and CSS) like we did before, you can read from that file and output the equivalent file name (the one with a content hash string), or you can even imagine that you have a helper method that reads from the manifest.json file and returns the hashed version of the file name that you can use in your HTML layout as follows:

```
<script src="build/<?php echo get_hashed_filename('application.js'); ">
</script>
```

Now that we have an idea about what the manifes.json file is, we still don't want to use it here for simplicity purposes (no need to add a server-side script or a framework stack just to demonstrate how to parse the manifest.json file and call it from our HTML). So the solution for now is to copy the name (that contains the hash string) of our desired JS/CSS file from the manifest.json and paste it manually in index.html as the source of the script or link tag.

## Alternative to Manifest

But wait, are we going to hard-code these links by hand and update them every single time the hash content of a file changes?

The answer is maybe yes, if you're not lazy. I won't do it myself anyway, and I would prefer to let webpack do that instead by creating an output index.html for us. Let's explore this alternative.

Instead of using the manifest.json file, there is a second option that we can use with the help of a plugin called htmlWebpackPlugin. The webpack documentation (https://webpack.js.org/plugins/html-webpack-plugin/) states that:

> *The HtmlWebpackPlugin simplifies creation of HTML files to serve your webpack bundles. This is especially useful for webpack bundles that include a hash in the filename which changes every compilation.*

Since we have JavaScript and CSS files with a hash that changes on compilation whenever we update our source files, this plugin seems to be exactly what we are looking for. Let's install:

```
$ npm install --save-dev html-webpack-plugin
```

The next step is to require it in the webpack.config.js file:

```
const HtmlWebpackPlugin = require('html-webpack-plugin');
```

Then to use it, all we have to do is add it to the plugins array as was done with the previous plugins:

```
plugins: [
  new HtmlWebpackPlugin(),
  // ...
]
```

Now let's run the command `npm run build` and check our build folder. Do you see something added in there? Yep! A new file "index.html" was generated and added to our "build" folder. It contains HTML code generated by webpack with a reference to the compiled CSS files as well as our JavaScript files (both application and admin), and you can see that the content hash we saw before was added as well. It is important to notice that the file under build folder (build/index.html) has no relation with the previously existing index.html file at the root of our project folder.

With that said, instead of opening the index.html located under root of our project folder, we will open the one created for us by webpack, which is located in the "build" folder. Try it and make sure everything is working as expected.

However, you still need one more thing to make this work perfectly. So far, Webpack created an index.html with nothing but a basic HTML code structure containing references to our bundled CSS and JS files, but if you have content (text or paragraphs or anything else) that you want to show on your page, there is no way until you tell webpack about it.

Using a custom template file, we will tell webpack to use an HTML skeleton that will be bundled into the index.html result file, and webpack will take care of it by adding the necessary html tags pointing to our stylesheets and JavaScript files so we don't need to worry about the name of these files every time the hash content changes.

Let's create a file "template.html" (you can name it whatever you like) under our "src" folder, and let's add some HTML content to it as shown in Listing 4-1.

***Listing 4-1.*** Creating a template for Webpack Html Plugin

```html
<!DOCTYPE html>
<html lang="en" dir="ltr">
  <head>
  <meta charset="utf-8">
  <title>My custom template</title>
</head>
<body>
  <p style="background:white;">
Lorem ipsum dolor sit amet, consectetur adipisicing elit, sed do eiusmod
tempor incididunt ut labore et dolore magna aliqua. Ut enim a d minim veniam,
quis nostrud exercitation ullamco laboris nisi ut aliq uip ex ea commodo
consequat. Duis aute irure dolor in reprehenderit in voluptate velit esse
cillum dolore eu fugiat nulla pariatur. Excepteur sint occaecat cupidatat non
proident, sunt in culpa qui officia dese runt mollit anim id est laborum.
```

```
    </p>
  </body>
</html>
```

Now we need to tell our `HTMLWebpackPlugin` to use that template to generate the index.html output. In the webpack.config.js file, we just need to add a "template" option to our plugin like this:

```
plugins: [
  new HtmlWebpackPlugin({
    template: './src/template.html'
  }),
  // ...
]
```

It's time to run webpack to get our bundle updated:

```
$ npm run build
```

Once completed, open index.html (remember: the one located under the build folder) in your browser, you can see that our "lorem ipsum" paragraph is there, and that our stylesheet and JavaScript tags were added as well as shown in Figure 4-9.

```
     index.html                 ×
 1   <!DOCTYPE html>
 2   <html lang="en" dir="ltr">
 3     <head>
 4     <meta charset="utf-8">
 5     <title>My custom template</title>
 6   <link href="application-990c4fefb9bb961c9b31.css" rel="stylesheet"><link
 •   href="admin-86770eec42ae6a2573dc.css" rel="stylesheet"></head>
 7   <body>
 8     <p style="background:white;">
 9   Lorem ipsum dolor sit amet, consectetur adipisicing elit, sed do\
10   eiusmod tempor incididunt ut labore et dolore magna aliqua. Ut enim a\
11   d minim veniam, quis nostrud exercitation ullamco laboris nisi ut aliq\
12   uip ex ea commodo consequat. Duis aute irure dolor in reprehenderit in\
13   voluptate velit esse cillum dolore eu fugiat nulla pariatur. Excepteu\
14   r sint occaecat cupidatat non proident, sunt in culpa qui officia dese\
15   runt mollit anim id est laborum.
16       </p>
17     <script type="text/javascript" src="application-813a48bef293e56f499c.js"></script><script
 •   type="text/javascript" src="admin-ca597cfb416c703f7945.js"></script></body>
18   </html>
19
```

***Figure 4-9.*** *The file build/index.html source after applying a template to HtmlWebpackPlugin*

As you can see, we no longer have to change the names of our JavaScript and CSS files (manually) whenever the content hash changes. By using `HtmlWebpackPlugin`, Webpack will take care of injecting the right tags with the corresponding file name for each resource. To ensure this is working correctly, make sure to open build/index.html in your browser instead of the index.html at the root of the project folder.

Finally, before we move on to the next chapter, and in order to avoid any confusion, I would suggest that you delete the old index.html (in the root folder) because we will use the build/index.html generated by `HtmlWebpackPlugin`.

# Summary

The benefit you get from using cache busting in any web application is significant, so it's one of the mandatory things you should consider when bundling your assets. We have explored many topics in this chapter, starting from naming and substituting our files names to cleaning the "build" folder, then ending by dynamically injecting the right (generated) files names to our HTML. In the next chapter, we will talk about something interesting when learning webpack: resolving folders. I hope you are still excited to learn more cool stuff. Let's jump in.

# CHAPTER 5

# Resolving Folders

After seeing how to prepare our file for caching and exploring the necessary plugins for that purpose, it's time to tackle a new chapter dedicated to folders: how to replace their path by aliases and how to resolve modules from them. It might seem like I'm saying something strange here, but you will understand what I mean in few minutes.

## Organizing Our Files

Before going straight to the main subject, let's do some organization. So far, all our source code was placed in one folder called "src," and all our compiled files go to the "build" folder. What we want to do here is organize our files better, and separate our JavaScript from our CSS from our images, so let's do that.

1) We are going to create three folders in our "src" folder: one called "javascripts," one called "stylesheets," and one called "images."

2) We are going to move our JavaScript files to the "javascripts" folder, our CSS/SCSS files to the "stylesheets" folder, and finally our image files to the "images" folder. You can see the new structure in Figure 5-1.

© Mohamed Bouzid 2020

M. Bouzid, *Webpack for Beginners*, https://doi.org/10.1007/978-1-4842-5896-5_5

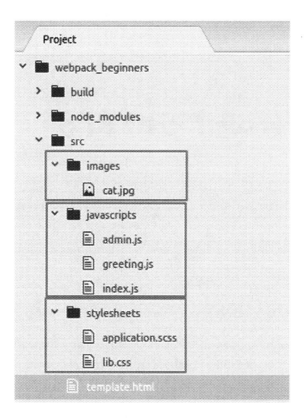

*Figure 5-1.* *Grouping files with same extension in organized folders*

Now that we have a new structure for our source files, we need to update our webpack.config.js in order to reflect that change. In the "entry" option, we need to add the "javascripts" folder to the path of our files:

```
entry: {
  application: "./src/javascripts/index.js",
  admin: "./src/javascripts/admin.js"
}
```

Let's call webpack to compile our files:

```
$ npm run build
```

Now if you check the terminal, you will see an error. Figure 5-2 shows the output of my terminal after calling the build command.

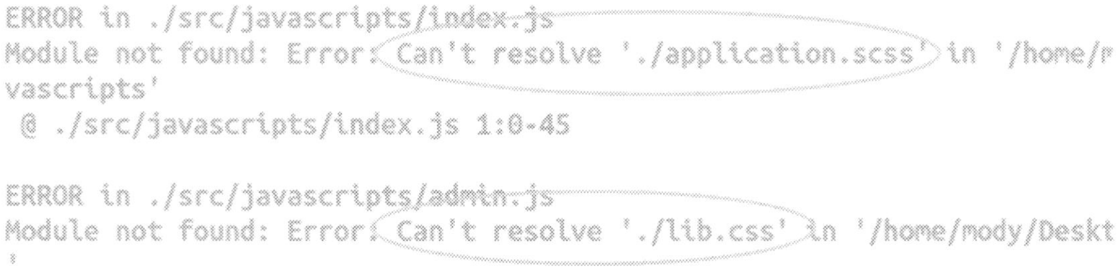

```
ERROR in ./src/javascripts/index.js
Module not found: Error: Can't resolve './application.scss' in '/home/r
vascripts'
 @ ./src/javascripts/index.js 1:0-45

ERROR in ./src/javascripts/admin.js
Module not found: Error: Can't resolve './lib.css' in '/home/mody/Deskt
```

***Figure 5-2.*** *Webpack can't resolve our CSS files after changing their location*

As you can see, the error says, "Can't resolve './application.scss'... and './lib.css'"; this makes sense because in our index.js file, we have this line:

```
import application from "./application.scss"
```

Which is no longer pointing to the right location, so let's go ahead and change it as follows:

```
import application from "../stylesheets/application.scss"
```

Same thing for lib.css in "admin.js." Here is the line after modification:

```
import lib from "../stylesheets/lib.css"
```

To prevent another error, adjust the path to "cat.jpg" in the "application.scss" file as well, for the following line:

```
background-image: url('cat.jpg');
```

The correct path to the image should be:

```
background-image: url('../images/cat.jpg');
```

Make sense? I hope so. Now if we compile our files using the ***"npm run build,"*** we will get everything working correctly.

# Aliases

The structure we used here is simple and recommended in most projects, but you might want to have a complex structure depending on the project you are working on. In our example, it was easy to refer to our CSS/SCSS file from our JS file; for example:

```
import application from "../stylesheets/application.scss."
```

But depending on the complexity of the nesting of your folders, you may end up using something like this:

```
import application from "../../../stylesheets/application.scss"
```

This is tedious to write, but of course I'm not encouraging you to use a complex folder structure in your project. In some situations, you may face things like that or maybe you are working on a legacy project that is structured in a horrible way. This is why I want to talk about something useful for these scenarios, which we call an "Alias" or "Aliases."

Aliases are useful when importing or requiring modules or files, so instead of using the above complex path, we can instead add a "`resolve.alias`" to our webpack.config. js, which points to our "stylesheets" folder:

```
module.exports = {
  //...
  resolve: {
    alias: {
      CssFolder: path.resolve(__dirname, 'src/stylesheets/')
    }
  }
}
```

Then when we import a CSS/SCSS file, i.e: application.scss, we can simply use:

```
import application from "CssFolder/application.scss"
```

Now, run the webpack command and make sure the output in the terminal is all green:

```
$ npm run build
```

As expected, everything is working perfectly. The only difference is that now the path is cleaner.

---

**Note**   Just for the sake of remembering, whenever you make a change to the configuration file, you should rerun the webpack (build) command, even if you are using the watch mode.

---

Aliases can be very handy for many situations. It's something you want to think about whenever you face a situation where you group your files in different subfolders or you just have some relative paths that look awful to type.

# Resolving Modules

While we are talking about the webpack "Alias" resolver, I want to mention another helpful resolver, which is "resolve.modules." What this does is tell webpack what directories it should be looking in when resolving modules.

By default, when doing something like importing a third-party library in one of our JavaScript files, for example, when importing jQuery we do:

```
import $ from 'jquery'
```

Webpack will look into the "node_modules" directory, which is equivalent to the resolving "node_modules" folder as seen below:

```
module.exports = {
  //...
  resolve: {
    alias: {
      CssFolder: path.resolve(__dirname, 'src/stylesheets/')
    },

    modules: ['node_modules']
  }
};
```

If we want to tell webpack to look in another directory before going to "node_modules" (let's imagine we have downloaded some JavaScript libraries manually and we have a folder called "**downloaded_libs**"), in this case we are going to specify that folder before the "node_modules" folder in the resolve.modules option.

```
module.exports = {
  // ...
  resolve: {
    alias: {
      CssFolder: path.resolve(__dirname, 'src/stylesheets/')
    },

    modules: [path.resolve(__dirname, 'src/downloaded_libs'), 'node_modules']
  },
};
```

Now webpack will look in "downloaded_libs" folder first, then if the module we are looking for doesn't exist there, it will continue the search in the "node_modules" folder, which is the "default."

To demonstrate this, let's create a folder named "downloaded_libs" under the "src" folder. Then, let's download the jQuery library file from `https://jquery.com/download/` and place it into the folder we have just created under the name of "jquery.js". Figure 5-3 shows the folder we created with the downloaded jquery file.

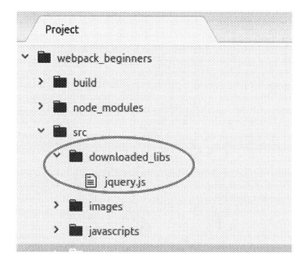

***Figure 5-3.*** *Creation of a separate folder to contain our third-party library (jquery.js)*

In our index.js file, let's import jQuery and use it to see if it's working. First, import it and always make sure that your imports are at the top of the file:

```
import application from "CssFolder/application.scss"
import { sayHello } from './greeting.js';
import $ from 'jquery';
```

You can use whatever alias you want. I'm using a dollar ($) sign here in order to refer to the jQuery object, because that's the convention for jQuery, but it's up to you if you prefer to use jQuery or jq or something else. Just make sure to call the proper alias; for example, instead of using *$('.selector')*, you will have to use your custom alias, like *jQuery('.selector')* or *jq('.selector')*, etc.

Note that we did not use a relative path (i.e., '../downloaded_libs/jquery') because as we discussed before, webpack is now able to look for the "downloaded_libs" folder automatically when importing modules.

Finally, to make sure the jQuery library was imported and it's working, let's add the following line to the end of index.js:

```
$('body').append('<div style="background:yellow;padding:10px;">Hello
jQuery!</div>');
```

What this line does is simply add a yellow styled DIV with a text "Hello jQuery!" to our page body. Open the terminal and call the webpack command:

```
$ npm run build
```

Go to your browser and see what index.html file looks like. Figure 5-4 shows the "hello jquery!" message added by jquery with the yellow background.

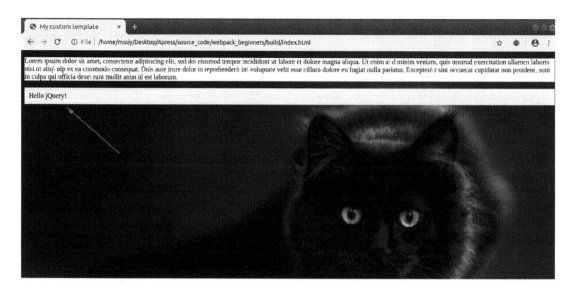

**Figure 5-4.** *Appending text via jquery using "resolve module" option*

You can see that it's possible for you to add a custom folder like we did and copy your third-party JavaScript libraries into it, then let webpack figure that out for you using the "*resolve.modules*" option. However you will miss the power of your package manager (npm or yarn), which you would prefer to use instead of downloading manually your libraries.

I have just shown you this option to be aware of it in case you want to use it for specific cases. But I would still recommend using npm or yarn to download your JavaScript libraries and import them in your code, we will talk more about this subject in the last chapter of this book.

If you have noticed a warning in your terminal about the bundled application-*. js file has exceeded the size limit as shown in Figure 5-5, don't worry. It's because the jQuery library was embedded into that file, which makes it obviously bigger.

```
WARNING in entrypoint size limit: The following
entrypoint(s) combined asset size exceeds the re
commended limit (244 KiB). This can impact web p
erformance.
Entrypoints:
  application (789 KiB)
      application-990c4fefb9bb961c9b31.css
      application-af0f4ead6c36b781ee73.js
```

***Figure 5-5.*** *Webpack warning about our application.js size limit*

For now, ignore this warning, it's really not that important, and not all warnings are bad, including this one. We will discuss more about this later.

## Summary

In this chapter, we have organized our files, seen the usage of aliases, and shown how to resolve modules from a custom folder. You can see now how flexible webpack is, and how you can make things organized in the way you want or prefer to. I hope in this chapter you learned something that will serve you in the future, as I'm sure there are many cases where you will need to refer back to the techniques described here. In the next chapter, we will explore Webpack Dev Server, which is a lightweight server that comes with webpack out of the box in order to make your development work easier.

# CHAPTER 6

# Webpack DevServer

Now it's time to talk about the webpack development server, which is mostly referred to as webpack-dev-server. We will explore the basic options and see how it will save us compilation time and give us a nice URL to work with. We will also learn about HMR (Hot Module Replacement), which will help us update our page without a full reload.

## Installing and Configuring Webpack Dev Server

So far, we have used the command "**npm run build**" *repeatedly in order to bundle our code.* Then to view the changes, we open the index.html file in the browser manually after locating that file first in our machine. In addition to that. keep in mind that when your files get bigger and/or you're adding more plugins or loaders to do certain tasks, you will notice that the compilation is taking more time to finish. Sometimes it's really slow, but the good news is that you don't have to suffer either waiting (at least after the first compilation) or searching for that index.html in your file system every time – there is a better way to do it: Webpack-Dev-Server.

Webpack provides us with a ready-to-use development web server, which will help us reduce our compilation time drastically, give us an HTTP URL to access our HTML page(s) from (rather than the file protocol), and can even recompile the bundle and reload our page whenever something gets changed in our JavaScript, CSS, etc.

The first step we have to do is to install webpack-dev-server:

```
$ npm install --save-dev webpack-dev-server
```

After the installation is done, let's open webpack.config.js and configure webpack-dev-server as follows:

```
module.exports = {
  devServer: {
    port: 9000,
```

© Mohamed Bouzid 2020
M. Bouzid, *Webpack for Beginners*, https://doi.org/10.1007/978-1-4842-5896-5_6

```
    contentBase: path.resolve(__dirname, 'build')
  },
  // ...
}
```

Here we have set a port (9000) for our server. You can set this to whatever you like; just make sure it's a free port that's not used by any of your running programs. The contentBase option role is to specify which folder should be used to serve the static content (I'm referring more precisely to the index.html file) from. In case it's not set, it will default to the root of the working directory. But in our case, even though we have set that option explicitly, it won't make any difference because we are using htmlWebpackPlugin, as a consequence the index.html file will be part of the webpack bundle, and **when using webpack-dev-server**, that bundle will be built and served from memory (which takes precedence over the local filesystem) regardless of the specified "contentBase" path. In case any file (HTML, JS, CSS, etc.) is not found in memory, webpack-dev-server will fall back on "contentBase" directory and tries to fetch that file.

So, in short, you need to retain this: webpack-dev-server loads and serves any bundled file from memory instead of the local filesystem. If any resource (HTML, JS, CSS, etc.) is not found in memory, webpack-dev-server will look at the "contentBase" path and try to find the missed file there. When no "contentBase" option is set, it will look at the root of the working directory.

---

**Note**    When specifying the contentBase option, Webpack recommends using an absolute path; that's why we relied on path.resolve in the snippet above. While it was my intention to make clear how the "contentBase" works, using it is optional. You may not need to use it in most cases.

---

I would like to remind you that so far, we were using "*npm run build*" to compile our files. It's the package.json that has made that command possible, which under the surface calls webpack itself:

```
"scripts": {
  "build": "webpack"
}
```

We are going to do the same thing by adding another script that will call webpack-dev-server whenever we run npm with a command like "start" or "serve" or any other word you like to use. I would prefer to use "start" here (referring to "start the server") as follows:

```
"scripts": {
  "build": "webpack",
  "start": "webpack-dev-server"
}
```

So let's try calling webpack-dev-server using the new command:

```
$ npm run start
```

Figure 6-1 shows the output of our terminal after starting our webpack-dev-server.

```
> webpack-dev-server

i ⌜wds⌟: Project is running at http://localhost:9000/
i ⌜wds⌟: webpack output is served from /
i ⌜wds⌟: Content not from webpack is served from /home/mody/Des
ktop/Apress/source_code/webpack_beginners/build
⚠⌜wdm⌟: Hash: b9583c5374604cbdb01d
Version: webpack 4.41.5
Time: 14075ms
```

***Figure 6-1.*** *Webpack-dev-server has started, and it tells us that it's running at* `http://localhost:9000/`

Webpack is started and running at port 9000. You can see that it says, "*webpack output is served from /*" which means that webpack is serving our bundle (JavaScript, CSS, etc.) from the root url "/" (related to the root web server), which is basically `http://localhost:9000/` and not from a subdirectory like `http://localhost:9000/subdirectory/`. You can also notice that it says, "Content not from webpack is served from .../build" which is where index.html is supposed to be, if it did not already exist in memory. Another way to explain "content not from webpack" is any static file that is not part of the webpack bundle.

In case you are curious and you want to verify that our bundle is served from memory, you can check the "build" folder (after starting the server) and make sure it's empty.

---

**Note**   I'm assuming here that you are using the CleanWebpackPlugin we saw previously, which cleans up the "build" folder every time before a new bundle is created. In case you are not using that plugin, the "build" folder may contain the old generated bundle (created when the "npm run build" command was used) but all the files in that bundle will remain unchanged across builds.

---

So whenever you see the expression, "Webpack output is served from /", this means that the bundle will be served from the root of the server, which is basically like a virtual location in the memory. This location can be changed using an option called publicPath, and we will talk more about it in the next section.

Let's open up the browser and type in the URL `http://localhost:9000` in the address bar, like shown in Figure 6-2. Our page is working as before but this time with a much cleaner URL.

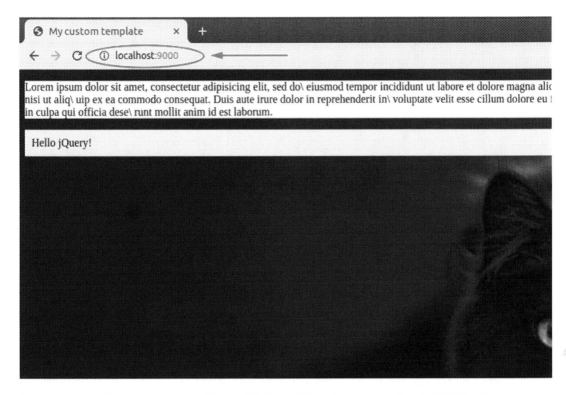

***Figure 6-2.*** *Our page served from WebpackDevServer under the URL of localhost:9000*

Also note that the server stays running, so we can go and edit/update things like the content of our HTML template or our CSS/JS source files. Then we will see that the content of our page gets reloaded whenever we make and save these changes because webpack will reflect those updates in memory instantly. This is cool but the page gets fully reloaded (which will take a little time) and if you have, for example, some kind of form on your page filled with data and then you decided to change something like a button background color, the whole page will get reloaded and your data will be gone once you save the source file. To solve this, we will be using a feature called the Hot Module Replacement. We will talk about HMR shortly.

# Understanding publicPath option

As we have just seen in the previous section, the webpack bundle is built and served from memory at the root url (/) of our server, which means that if we have

an application.js file, we can access it in the browser at the url `http://localhost:9000/`
`application.js`. That's because webpack-dev-server has a "`publicPath`" option that is
by default set to '/'.

Sometimes, we want to serve our static files under a specific folder like "assets" or
"statics" etc. In this case, we just need to set the devServer.publicPath option to the
desired folder as follows:

```
devServer: {
  port: 9000,
  contentBase: path.resolve(__dirname, 'build'),
  publicPath: '/assets/'
}
```

Now the application.js file will be available virtually (in memory) under a folder "/
assets/" and we can access it from `http://localhost:9000/assets/application.js`.

Let's try the above configuration (do not forget to re-run the "npm run start"
command after that) and see what will happen when we visit the root url `http://`
`localhost:9000`.

Oops! Our index.html page disappeared and all we see is an empty page with a sign
similar to this "~ /". This indicates that there is nothing at the root of the server. How that
can be?

It's because we are using `htmlWebpackPlugin` which makes the generated index.
html part of the webpack bundle. As you may have guessed, our bundle is (virtually) no
longer under the root "/" but under "/assets/" (after we used the `publicPath` option),
which means that index.html is too located under "/assets/" folder. You can prove this by
visiting `http://localhost:9000/assets/index.html`

Does webpack-dev-server try to fallback to something when no index.html was
found in the server root? Yes, it does fallback to the "`contentBase`" path which is the
"build" folder, but as this folder is empty, there is nothing to show there. In case you're
curious, go ahead and create a dummy index.html (with some dummy content) in
the "build" folder and then refresh the page (without restarting the server) at `http://`
`localhost:9000` to see that this time it will use the HTML file you have just created.

With all that in mind, the `publicPath` option makes more sense when used
with an index.html not generated as part of the bundle (like it's the case with
`htmlWebpackPlugin`), but more practically when used with an index file that is generated
by a programming language in conjunction with the manifest.json file (we talked about

manifest.json in chapter 4) in order to get the name of each bundled file and have it proceeded by the publicPath folder name i.e:

```
<script src="./assets/<?= getBundleFileName(); ?>"></script>
```

One last thing to know is that there is a similar option to devServer.pubicPath, but for the output configuration called also publicPath (output.publicPath) and it's recommended that devServer.publicPath is the same as output.publicPath in case the later one is used.

Before we move to the next section, make sure you delete or comment out the "publicPath" option as we are not going to use here. I just wanted you to be aware of it and understand how it's used in case you may need it in the future.

# Hot Module Replacement

Sometimes we need to apply a few changes to certain elements in the page like changing the color, the text, or the position of a button, etc., and we want these changes to be reflected in the page immediately without fully reloading it. That's when HMR (Hot Module Replacement) comes into play; it works out of the box with webpack and fortunately it's easy to activate.

HMR depends on a plugin called "webpack HotModuleReplacementPlugin," but webpack makes it even easier for us to use by just adding an extra option to the configuration file. That option will add the necessary plugin for us, and no extra step is required from our part as described in the documentation:

> *Note that webpack.HotModuleReplacementPlugin is required to fully enable HMR. If webpack or webpack-dev-server are launched with the --hot option, this plugin will be added automatically, so you may not need to add this to your webpack.config.js. See the HMR concepts page for more information.*

So all we have to do is to add (hot: true) to the devServer configuration in webpack.config.js as follows:

```
devServer: {
  port: 9000,
  contentBase: path.resolve(__dirname, 'build'),
  hot: true
}
```

And voilà! You have just added the HMR power to your webpack-dev-server.

---

**Note**    It's totally possible to append the --hot option to the server call in our package.json under "scripts" for the line ("start": "webpack-dev-server --hot") so that the command "npm run start" runs the server with HMR enabled.

---

After either setting the option "hot" to true or adding the "--hot" flag to the webpack-dev-server command call like noted above, let's jump into the terminal and start the server in order to see what will happen:

```
$ npm run start
```

An unexpected error message shows up! As seen in Figure 6-3, It seems that the HMR doesn't like the [contenthash] we used before to output filenames.

```
ERROR in chunk admin [entry]
admin-86770eec42ae6a2573dc.css
Cannot use [chunkhash] or [contenthash] for chunk in '[name]-[c
ontenthash].js' (use [hash] instead)

ERROR in chunk application [entry]
application-990c4fefb9bb961c9b31.css
Cannot use [chunkhash] or [contenthash] for chunk in '[name]-[c
ontenthash].js' (use [hash] instead)
```

***Figure 6-3.*** *HMR complains about contenthash substitution*

What that error tells us basically is to use [hash] instead of using [chunkhash] or [contenthash]. This issue is related to the usage of [contenthash] in conjunction with webpack-dev-server and it's caused by the "hot" option we used previously in our devServer configuration. While the reason behind this is not officially documented by webpack, it's reported that using it causes many other issues, like memory leak and also because the devServer does not know when to clean up the old cached files. To avoid any issue, it's recommended to turn caching off in development and use it only for the production mode in which we won't need to use webpack-dev-server anyway.

In case you are wondering what's the difference between [hash], [chunkhash], and [contenthash], a brief explanation follows.

On one hand, the substitution [hash] will generate the same hash string for the bundled files across every build, the generated hash is based on our source files together, that means if we change something in one file, a new hash will be generated and all bundled files' names will be set with this new hash. In production, when something changes, this will result in the browser not only downloading the specific file that got updated but all the other files as well regardless if they got updated or not.

On the other hand, [chunkhash] is based on every chunk. For example, if you have a file index.js where you imported index.css and you have another file admin.js where you imported admin.css, this will result on application-*.js and application-*.css having the same hash because they are the result of the same chunk "application." However, admin-*.js and admin-*.css have a different hash (but are identical for both) because they are coming from another chunk "admin." If you update the content of admin.css (which is part of the chunk "admin"), a new hash will be generated and both admin-*. css and admin-*.js will get the same new hash without affecting or changing the hash of application-*.css and application-*.js.

Last, the [contenthash] is calculated based on each file content separately, which means if the content of a file changes, only that file will get a different hash when bundled. Easy to understand, isn't it?

Every situation is different and there are use cases where you want to use [hash] or [chunkhash] but in production, for most cases you would use [contenthash].

---

**Note**   All the types of hashes can be shortened using two colons followed by a number that represents the desired length, that is, [contenthash:6], [hash:8], [chunkhash:5], etc. ...

---

Now that we have an idea about the different hashes we can use and how each one is generated, let's try and fix the error we have faced above in our terminal. But just before that, my suggestion to you is to create a variable that contains the mode we are working on (development or production) and use that variable instead of hard-coding the value itself, so instead of using:

```
module.exports = {
  mode: "development",
  // ...
}
```

I would prefer to do something like:

```
// ...
const mode = "development";
module.exports = {
  mode: mode,
  // ...
}
```

Then to solve the issue that we have just seen, we are going to use [contenthash] only for production while using [hash] or even better not using caching at all in development mode. So here is how I do it in my webpack.config.js file:

```
output: {
  filename: mode === 'production' ? "[name]-[contenthash].js" : '[name].js',
  // ...
}
```

With that conditional line, the contenthash will be used only for production mode. Let's do the same for the MiniCssExtractPlugin as follows:

```
plugins: [
  // ...
  new MiniCssExtractPlugin({
    filename: mode === 'production' ? "[name]-[contenthash].css" :
    '[name].css',
  })
]
```

---

**Note**  For the HMR to work later… avoid adding any hash to MiniCssExtractPlugin in "development" mode

---

The same applies to the "url-loader" configuration:

```
test: /\.(png|jpg|gif|svg)$/i,
use: [
  {
    loader: 'url-loader ',
```

```
  options: {
    // ...
    name: mode === "production" ? "[name]-[hash:7].[ext]" : "[name].[ext]"
  }
 }
]
```

Make sure your "mode" variable is set to "development," and once everything is set up correctly, all you have to do is start the webpack server:

```
$ npm run start
```

Now try to update something in your JS or CSS. In my case, I'm going to change the yellow (I have set using jQuery) in my index.js file to another color, like "green," for example:

```
$('body').append('<div style="background:green;padding:10px;">Hello
jQuery!</div>');
```

You can add/edit anything, or just change yellow to green like I did. Then save the file while keeping an eye open in your browser to see what will happen to the page.

As you may notice, the page reloaded, however FULLY! This is not what we are aiming for. We want to update only the part that was changed, but the whole page was reloaded – which is equivalent to refreshing the browser tab. Note that it may take a few seconds to see the page reloading but if the page doesn't get reloaded like expected, you can refresh it manually for the first time then start editing and testing your files.

While the page is getting refreshed, the browser's console is trying to tell us why the reloading part is not working as expected, but the message disappeared so quickly because of how console logs are configured by default in the browser's developer tools. To find out more about the issue, we are going to make our console logs persistent from page to page, and that will help us see why the HMR is not working as expected.

If you are using Mozilla Firefox, then open your console and click the gear icon, then click the "Persist Logs" as shown in Figure 6-4.

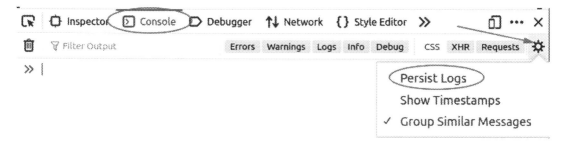

**Figure 6-4.** *Persisting log under Mozilla Firefox*

The same thing applies to Google Chrome browser. You have to open your console, click on the "gear" icon at the top right corner, and a list of options will appear. Check the "Preserve log" check box as shown in Figure 6-5.

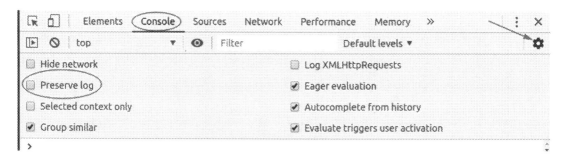

**Figure 6-5.** *Persisting log under Google Chrome*

---

**Note**    Depending on the browser you are using and its current version, you may have a slightly different user interface than mine, but the principle remains the same.

---

Now that our logs are ready to be persisted from page to page (or from refresh to refresh), let's edit the index.js file and change the "green" we have set previously to "orange" like this:

```
$('body').append('<div style="background:orange;padding:10px;">Hello
jQuery!</div>');
```

When we save, the page will be reloaded fully like before, but we are able to see the warning of the issue clearly in the browser console. As shown in Figure 6-6, the warning says, "*Aborted because ./src/javascripts/index.js is not accepted.*"

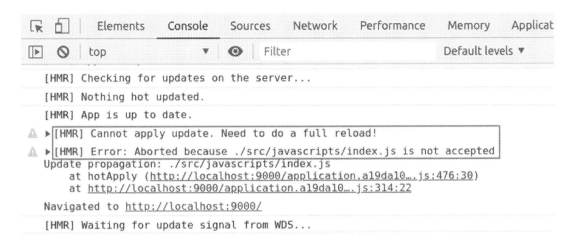

**Figure 6-6.** *Hot Module Reload warning as it falls back to a full reload*

What this means is that our index.js is not accepting hot updates because we haven't instructed it to do so. That's why it falls back to full page reloading!

To fix this, we just need to add the simple following code to the end of the "src/javascripts/index.js" file:

```
if (module.hot) {
  module.hot.accept(function (err) {
    console.log(err);
  });
}
```

The callback function we have passed as an argument to `module.hot.accept()` is optional, and it can be used in case an error happens and you want to log it or do something else.

Once done, reload the page and start making some changes to your source code. The Hot Module Reload will start functioning as expected. One thing to note though is that if you're using something like jQuery *append* method that we have been playing with previously, you will notice that the appended div (or any element you are appending) will show in the page and whenever you change something in index.js file, all the code in that file will get executed again, which will recall the append method one more time; and a new DIV will be added to our page body while keeping the older appended DIV there. In Figure 6-7, you will see what I ended up with by changing the color of the div appended by jquery from yellow to orange (the one saying "Hello jQuery!").

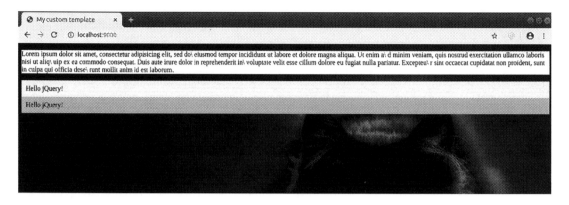

***Figure 6-7.*** *HMR: A new div appended when editing the "div" color in jquery append method, resulting in having two appended DIVs*

You are maybe saying this is not what I'm expecting but re-executing all the code in the updated file is how HMR works with JavaScript. There is a "Gotchas" section in the webpack documentation if you want to explore more at `https://webpack.js.org/guides/hot-module-replacement/#gotchas` where it explains exactly that, and what they did in the example is that they removed the elements added using some JavaScript within the "module.hot.accept. I won't go deep into this because it's out of the scope of this book and also it's not the most important thing you have to worry about because mostly you will have HMR already set up for you within the web framework you are using instead of the one provided by webpack. But in case you are using webpack as a stand-alone solution, then feel free to check the example provided in the documentation.

However, with CSS, there is no such issue like with JavaScript. You will see that the HMR will work fine; you just need to add (hmr: true) to `MiniCssExtractPlugin.loader` so the line:

```
MiniCssExtractPlugin.loader
```

has to be changed to the following form in order to add the "hmr" option:

```
{
  loader: MiniCssExtractPlugin.loader,
  options: {
    hmr: true,
  },
}
```

This should be done for both CSS and SCSS rules as shown in Listing 6-1.

***Listing 6-1.*** Enabling HMR for MiniCssExtractPlugin in CSS and SCSS Rules

```
module: {
  rules: [
    // ...
    {
      test: /\.css$/i,
      use: [
        {
          loader: MiniCssExtractPlugin.loader,
          options: {
            hmr: true,
          },
        }
        // ...


      ]
    },
    {
      test: /\.scss$/i,
      use: [
        {
          loader: MiniCssExtractPlugin.loader,
          options: {
            hmr: true,
          },
        }
        // ...
      ],
    },
  ]
}
```

I know that I'm pushing everything in one config file, which might not be the best solution. You might want to separate your webpack configuration file into two separate files with different names: one for development and another one for production. If you prefer to do so, then in your package.json file, you can set them as follows:

```
"scripts": {
  "build": "webpack",
  "dev": "webpack-dev-server --hot --config ./webpack.dev.config.js"
  "prod": "webpack-dev-server --config ./webpack.prod.config.js"
}
```

But in our case, let's keep everything in one file. We won't need to do more configurations than that; just go to your terminal and start webpack-dev-server again:

```
$ npm run start
```

Go this time to application.scss under "src/stylesheets" and let's remove the body background image:

```
background-image: url('../images/cat.jpg');
```

Save and verify that your page background image disappeared without reloading the entire page. You can add more style like setting another background image or changing the text color. Every change you make will be updated without the need of full reloading.

There are many other options we can add to the webpack-dev-server configuration like, for example, the "overlay" option:

```
devServer: {
  // ...
  overlay: true
}
```

This will tell webpack devServer to show errors straight in your web browser on an overlay popup whenever something wrong occurs; this way you won't need to go and check your terminal every time, which is very handy.

# Summary

In this chapter, we have seen the main options for webpack-dev-server, how to use it, and how to activate the HMR (Hot Module Replacement) in order to update the page without fully reloading. Also, an important thing to remember is that the webpack-dev-server is built for development purposes only, NOT as a production server. So, in any case, it isn't meant to replace a true classic web server. Other than that, you can go to the webpack documentation website and learn additional options if you are interested to know more. In the next chapter, we will explore the installation and usage of third-party libraries, which will be the final lesson in this journey, so let's jump right in.

## CHAPTER 7

# Installing Third-Party Libraries

Installing third-party libraries is confusing for a lot of beginners, especially when they don't know anything about webpack. But it isn't hard once you understand how to do it. In this chapter, we will see how to install some of the most common JavaScript libraries. Along the way, we will explore some tips and tricks you can use to install any other library you want beyond the listed examples. Finally, we will see how to use the lazy loading method to import libraries on demand in order to optimize our application.

## Welcome Isolation, Goodbye Global Variables

We have seen that in order to separate our code in different files, we used the export/ import syntax (to export it from one file, and import it in another one). This allows us to have a more organized code in what we call "modules" in JavaScript.

Also, for the sake of remembering, we have seen that when importing a third-party library, for example, "jQuery," all we have to do is:

```
import $ from "jquery"
```

Importing "jquery" like above (without specifying any path to it) is how we tell webpack to find jquery.js file in the node_modules folder, which is the default folder webpack uses to resolve the third-party libraries we are importing in our JavaScript files. However, specifying a relative path to a library is totally possible, whether located in node_modules itself or in another folder; but for libraries we install via NPM or Yarn, the syntax above is the way to go.

If you remember what we did previously in Chapter 5 when we talked about resolving folders, in order to use jQuery … we downloaded it manually from the official

97

M. Bouzid, *Webpack for Beginners*, https://doi.org/10.1007/978-1-4842-5896-5_7

website to a folder we named "downloaded_libs," and then we told webpack to resolve all modules in that folder as follows:

```
resolve: {
  // ...
  modules: [path.resolve(__dirname, 'src/downloaded_libs'), 'node_modules']
}
```

In this case, if we import jQuery in any file using (import $ from "jquery"), webpack will try to find it first in the "downloaded_libs" folder before moving to node_modules. This just shows you another possibility in case you have a custom folder with certain libraries that you want to resolve, but you don't want to install via a package manager! Now that we know some different ways to import a third-party library like jQuery, let's see how to install it.

Downloading JavaScript libraries manually is what developers used to do for a long time. In fact, many still do it that way, but time has evolved and JavaScript package managers such as NPM and Yarn (an NPM alternative created by Facebook) weren't invented for no reason, and the benefits you get from using these tools are much better compared to the first method. All you have to do is to open your terminal, make sure you are in the root of your project folder, then run the following NPM command:

```
$ npm install jquery
```

Or using Yarn, you can just do:

```
$ yarn add jquery
```

Don't forget to remove jquery.js file from "downloaded_libs" folder because we won't need it anymore. We will use a JavaScript package manager in order to download all the libraries we need like we just did above. In my case, I will continue to use NPM throughout the examples.

Once the installation finishes, let's open up our node_modules folder and try to locate the jquery file on it. Figure 7-1 shows the jquery folder under node_modules.

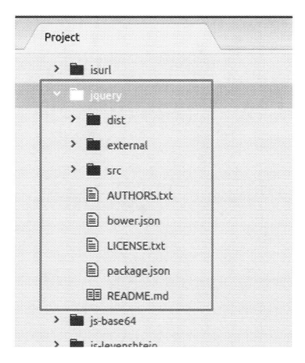

***Figure 7-1.***  *jQuery installed under node_modules folder*

But do you remember how we imported jQuery before in our index.js file? In case you don't, it was as follows:

```
import $ from "jquery"
```

If you're like me, I used to wonder how the above line knows about jquery file location without the need to specify the exact path to it?

Webpack seems to look by default into the node_modules folder (like we discussed previously) and tries to find a child folder with the same name as the imported library ("jquery" in this case), but how does it know exactly which file should be imported? After all, the folder of a third-party library may contain many other subfolders and files! In Figure 7-2, you can see part of the jquery folder structure that shows the location of the main jQuery files.

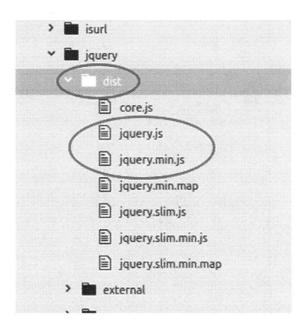

***Figure 7-2.*** *Location of jquery file under node_modules/jquery/dist*

Notice that there is a dist folder inside the "node_modules/jquery/" folder. This is where jQuery files are (we have a non-minified "jquery.js" file as well as a minified version "jquery.min.js"), so if you are still wondering how webpack knows that "dist/" is the folder where the jquery.js file is located, then take a look at package.json under "node_modules/jquery/". Figure 7-3 shows the exact line I'm referring to in that file.

***Figure 7-3.*** *A file package.json is delivered with most third-party libraries with a "main" key/entry*

By searching in the package.json file, you will be able to find a line that indicates the "main" file Webpack should pick when importing jQuery:

```
"main": "dist/jquery.js"
```

In this case the main file is jquery.js under the "dist" folder, but keep in mind that it's possible sometimes to find a JavaScript library or a plugin that isn't well written for the modern JavaScript world, which means it's possible to not find the package.json file at all; but fortunately, in most cases, you will.

---

**Note**   In case the third-party library you installed doesn't include a package.json file, you can use a relative path to import it from node_modules (i.e., import lib from "../node_modules/lib_folder/lib.js").

---

Now, suppose you already deleted jquery.js file from the "downloaded_libs" folder like I suggested earlier and you used a package manager to install jQuery. Let's go to the terminal and start webpack-dev-server and then make sure everything is working (jQuery should exist) like before by opening the URL http://localhost:9000 in the browser:

```
$ npm run start
```

The thing I want you to know at this point is even if we imported jquery in src/index. js, trying to access from outside that file would be impossible (thanks to webpack, global variables don't exist anymore). To demonstrate this case, I'm going to use jquery in the greeting.js file as shown in Listing 7-1.

***Listing 7-1.***  Using jQuery code inside greeting.js

```
export function sayHello(){
  // ...
  $('body').append('<div style="background:#EEE;">does jQuery exist here?
  </div>');
}
```

If you still remember, the function above is imported in index.js as follows:

```
import { sayHello } from './greeting';
import $ from 'jquery'
// ...
sayHello();
```

Note also that we are importing jQuery after importing the sayHello function so you might be thinking, "Well, we should import jQuery before it in order to make it accessible by that function," right?

Not exactly. That's how we used to think and do when we were using libraries that were exposed to the global scope, but with webpack, whatever you import in one file won't be accessible by another one. Each file is encapsulated and closed on its own. To prove this to you, let's move the importation of jQuery before importing sayHello like this:

```
// ...
import $ from 'jquery'
import { sayHello } from './greeting';
```

Start the server if it's not already started:

```
$ npm run start
```

Open the console of your browser and see the log error. As shown in Figure 7-4, an Uncaught ReferenceError was thrown, which explains that $ is not defined.

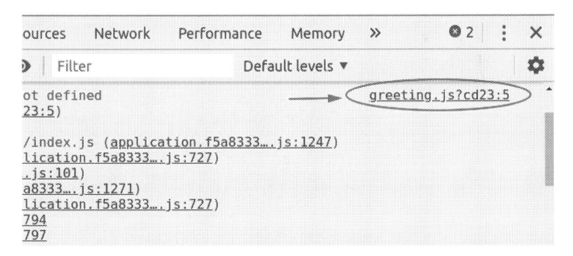

*Figure 7-4.* *Error showing the lack of jQuery library in greeting.js even after changing the order of imports*

You can even click the source line to see where that error comes from. As shown in Figure 7-5, the source of the error is in the right-side corner of the error message you get in the console.

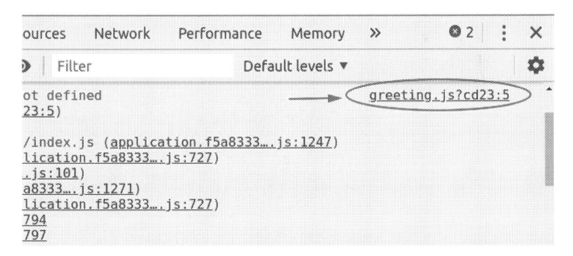

*Figure 7-5.* *A source map link that indicates which line the error is coming from*

Thanks to the source map we saw earlier in Chapter 3, clicking that will take us to the source of the error, which is self-explanatory.

The file greeting.js cannot find jQuery, so what now? The solution is simple, as shown in Listing 7-2; you should import it there too.

***Listing 7-2.*** Importing jQuery at the top of greeting.js

```
// import jquery
import $ from 'jquery'

function sayHello(){
  let tool = 'webpack';
  alert(`Hello I am ${tool}, welcome to ES6`);
  console.log('Can you find me?');
  $('body').append('<div style="background:#EEE;">does jQuery exist here?
  </div>');
}
//...
```

Doing this will make jQuery accessible in greeting.js, but don't worry. This doesn't mean that jQuery code will be copied twice in your final code. It just means that webpack will handle it to make it usable in both places while including it once in your code.

Now, if you go to your browser `http://localhost:9000`, you can see that the HTML we appended (using jQuery) in our greeting.js appears in the page as shown in Figure 7-6.

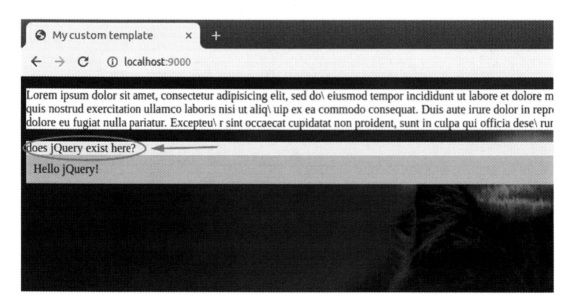

***Figure 7-6.*** *The appended message proves that jquery is working from greeting.js file*

What if we have a third file where we need jQuery? The answer is the same: just import jQuery in that file and it will work. For a case like this where there is a need to use a library like jQuery frequently in multiple files, there is a better way to do it. We will see this next.

## Using Bootstrap with Webpack

What about installing another library like Bootstrap? Can you guess what we need to do? First, we need to install it using our package manager NPM (or Yarn alternatively) from the terminal:

```
$ npm install bootstrap
```

Once Bootstrap is installed, we will need to import both bootstrap.css and bootstrap. js files. There is a *package.json* file that guides webpack to find which file is used mainly to import bootstrap, but that's for bootstrap.js only; we still need the styling (bootstrap. css) file. Figure 7-7 shows the main entry for Bootstrap.

*Figure 7-7.* *Bootstrap: The main entry in package.json*

For the CSS, we have to specify the path to bootstrap.css. In case you're not sure where it's located, you just need to explore node_modules/bootstrap/ folder and from there, you can explore more until you find it. To import bootstrap.css, use the following:

```
// import ...
import 'bootstrap/dist/css/bootstrap.css';
```

By adding this to our index.js file, we can now add something that's bootstrap related like a button with a class "btn-primary" to our template.html file under the text paragraph we created before:

```
<p>Lorem ipsum...</p>
<a href="#" class="btn btn-primary">button</a>
```

Save and then open the URL http://localhost:9000 in your browser. Figure 7-8 shows that the button we have added is styled with the "primary" color of bootstrap.

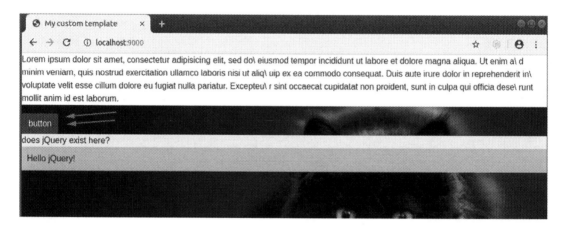

***Figure 7-8.*** *Bootstrap style applied to the button*

Now it's time to import bootstrap.js in our index.js, which should be straightforward, as you may remember the way we used to import jQuery was as follows:

```
import $ from 'jquery'
```

We should do something similar with Bootstrap, right? Something like this:

```
import bootstrap from 'bootstrap'
```

However, that's not true at some point, as there is a little exception here; bootstrap.js should be imported simply like this:

```
import 'bootstrap';
```

Do you see the difference? The reason is that Bootstrap JS is a ***jquery plugin***, and jQuery plugins just add functionalities to jQuery, which means they don't return anything for us but just extend jQuery's prototype, so no need to import the library in a variable (like we did for the $ variable with jQuery).

We know that every file/module is isolated on its own, and in the index.js file we are importing jQuery, then we are importing Bootstrap as the following:

```
import $ from 'jquery'
// ...
import 'bootstrap';
```

But how does the Bootstrap module know about our existing jQuery here, and how it's possible for it to add things to that exact jQuery instance?

If you see how bootstrap.js is written, you will find that it detects if we are in a modular environment like webpack, and if so it will **require** jQuery and Popper JS as shown in Figure 7-9, which is equivalent to the "import" method we used to import our libraries and files. (Remember that "import" is ES6 syntax while "require" is a similar function but it's a NodeJS syntax.)

```
 bootstrap.js                    ×
 6   (function (global, factory) {
 7     typeof exports === 'object' && typeof module !== 'undefined' ? factory(exports,
 •     require('jquery'), require('popper.js')) :
 8     typeof define === 'function' && define.amd ? define(['exports', 'jquery', 'poppe
 9     (global = global || self, factory(global.bootstrap = {}, global.jQuery, global.P
10   }(this, (function (exports, $, Popper) { 'use strict';
11
12     $ = $ && $.hasOwnProperty('default') ? $['default'] : $;
13     Popper = Popper && Popper.hasOwnProperty('default') ? Popper['default'] : Popper
```

***Figure 7-9.*** *Bootstrap.js: importing jQuery and Popper js if "exports" is an object (which is the case when using webpack)*

Because we already imported jQuery in the same file that bootstrap was imported to, webpack is smart enough to know this, so it will use that same jQuery instance we have imported, then it will apply the bootstrap plugin to it.

To make sure bootstrap.js is working, let's add another button to the template.html file and apply a tooltip to it (which is based on boostrap.js) as follows:

```
<button type="button" class="btn btn-secondary" data-toggle="tooltip" data-placement="top" title="Tooltip on top">Tooltip on top</button>
```

Then in src/index.js, we need to apply the tooltip to all the elements with [data-toggle="tooltip"] (don't try it yet unless you read the next paragraph) after importing Bootstrap as shown in the highlighted line below:

```
// ...
import 'bootstrap';

$('[data-toggle="tooltip"]').tooltip();
```

If we look closely in our terminal, there is an error stating that *it can't resolve popper.js*, which is a dependency of Bootstrap JS and it's needed in order to make the tooltip work properly. If you already activated the overlay option (overlay: true) within webpack devServer configuration, then the error will pop up in your browser as well, which makes debugging fun. Figure 7-10 shows the overlay error message in my browser.

***Figure 7-10.*** *Error overlay shows up because bootstrap needs popper.js*

The source of that error is the bootstrap.js; that's where popper.js is required, so that makes sense because it's not installed yet in our node modules. Let's install popper JS using the package manager NPM in our terminal:

```
$ npm install popper.js
```

At the moment of writing this, Bootstrap requires popper.js (the version 1) but that version is marked as deprecated, and the installation output from the terminal shows that a new version 2 is available. Because bootstrap hasn't updated the required PopperJS version yet to support the version 2, I will continue using the old version (popper.js), which is not that bad. Once Bootstrap updates the reference to the new version, then all you have to do is to install "@popperjs/core" instead.

---

**Note**   A package name might change over time if their owner(s) or maintainer(s) decided to. For example, until recently, the popperjs package name was "popper.js" (for the version 1.x), and then it has been deprecated in favor of a new version (v2) where the package name currently is "@popperjs/core." In order to get the name of the latest version, I would recommend you check the official package website.

---

Once installed, we need to start our webpack-dev-server again, and you'll see that our compilation succeeded this time:

```
$ npm run start
```

All you have to do now is to open the URL http://localhost:9000 in your browser (as you used to) and notice that the "tooltip" button is there. If you mouse over it, you will see a tooltip show up.

Like with jQuery, if you need to use bootstrap.js functions in any other file, you have to import it first. You may think that Bootstrap is already plugged in to jQuery so we can use it in other files like in greeting.js without importing it, but this won't work because it was applied only to the jQuery instance we have in our index.js. This means if you need to use something like the tooltip function from your greeting.js, you need to explicitly import Bootstrap.

We won't probably need to import Bootstrap frequently, for jQuery we surely do, but we don't want to import it in every file every time we need it. We need somehow to have it available for us in every file/module we write. That's when the webpack providePlugin comes into play.

# Webpack ProvidePlugin

There is a helpful plugin that will help us to make jQuery available in all our project source files called the providePlugin. which you can learn more about at `https://webpack.js.org/plugins/provide-plugin`.

Here is a brief description from the Webpack ProvidePlugin documentation:

> *Automatically load modules instead of having to import or require them everywhere.*

So, in our case, we will set up the ProvidePlugin in the configuration file (webpack.config.js) to load jQuery for us whenever there is a dollar sign ($) or jQuery object. Listing 7-3 shows us how to add the ProvidePlugin.

---

**Note**    The ProvidePlugin is shipped out of the box with webpack so you don't have to install it yourself.

---

***Listing 7-3.*** Usage of Webpack Provide Plugin

```
// ...
// make sure you require "webpack"
const webpack = require('webpack');

module.exports = {
  // ...
  plugins: [
    new webpack.ProvidePlugin({
      $: 'jquery',
      jQuery: 'jquery'
    }),
    // ...
  ]
  // ...
}
```

Since ProvidePlugin is part of webpack, all we have to do is require webpack, then call ProvidePlugin method on it in order to create a new instance of that plugin. What the code above will do is whenever there is a module that uses $ or jQuery variables, a code like the following will be added to that module file:

```
const $ = jQuery = require('jquery');
```

That's really useful for us because we will probably use jQuery in every JS file we create, but it will be helpful in other situations as well, especially when utilizing third-party plugins or libraries that expect jQuery as a global variable. Webpack has got you covered in this situation.

Note that we can also add the lines below to our Webpack ProvidePlugin in order to have jQuery available in our window or global object:

```
new webpack.ProvidePlugin({
  // ...
  "window.jQuery": "jquery'",
  "window.$": "jquery"
})
```

However, the window object here is meant to be for the build-time (for the libraries/dependencies that need `window.$` during the build phase) not for the run-time (meaning you won't be able to access $ in your browser console or in your HTML files). If you need jQuery to be exposed globally during the run-time don't use the above way but instead, add the following to one of your modules:

```
window.$ = window.jQuery = $
```

At the end it's up to you whether you want to expose jQuery to the window object or just make it available within your JavaScript modules only.

If you remember, we have imported bootstrap.css in index.js file as follows:

```
import 'bootstrap/dist/css/bootstrap.css';
```

While this is okay, what most people prefer to do is to have all CSS files imported and grouped in one single CSS file and have it imported by a JavaScript file. In our case, we will use the **src/application.scss** file to import bootstrap.css and any other CSS file, but there is a little detail to be aware of. Open the application.scss and add the following line at the top of the file:

```
@import '~bootstrap/dist/css/bootstrap.css';
```

Adding this line means that you need to **remove the importation of bootstrap.css from index.js**, so make sure to remove the following line before we continue:

```
import 'bootstrap/dist/css/bootstrap.css';
```

Back now to the new "import" we have made in our application.scss and note how the syntax is slightly different:

- The first thing is that the "import" keyword is preceded with an @, which is the standard way of importing CSS files in a SCSS file.

- The second thing is the tilde ~ before the word "bootstrap"; the reason for it is to tell webpack that we are importing a CSS located in node_modules.

What if we want to import a CSS file that is located within the stylesheets folder instead of a third-party CSS located within node modules? In this case the tilde ~ shouldn't be added, but a relative path to the file like this:

```
@import './another_css_file.css';
```

The dot (.) in the line above is to tell webpack that the CSS file is located in the same folder as application.scss. After importing many CSS files, you will end up with many imports (of different CSS files) as seen in Listing 7-4.

***Listing 7-4.*** Example of importing many CSS in application.scss

```
@import '~bootstrap/dist/css/bootstrap.css';
@import './another_css_file1.css';
@import './another_css_file2.css';
// ...
```

And the only import of CSS we will have in our index.js file will be the following one:

```
import application from "CssFolder/application.scss"
```

Remember that the "CssFolder" above is the alias we have given to our "src/stylesheets" in the webpack configuration file. With that in place, you can organize your code in a more efficient way by having your CSS file imported and grouped in one place. Now let's move on to install another JavaScript library.

# Installing jQuery-UI

Another jQuery plugin that we are going to install is jQuery UI, which is a well-known library and largely used by many websites. The principle of usage will be the same as what we have seen with bootstrap.js – to install jQuery-ui, we need first to run the following command in our terminal:

```
$ npm install jquery-ui
```

After the installation is done, let's import jQuery UI in our index.js file as follows:

```
// ...
import 'bootstrap';
import 'jquery-ui';
```

Everything looks fine so far, but if we wish to use one of the jQuery UI widgets, we will need to import that specific widget, too, in order to make it work. For example, there is a widget called "datepicker" in jQuery-ui, and if you want to use it you have to import it explicitly as follows:

```
// ...
import 'jquery-ui';
import 'jquery-ui/ui/widgets/datepicker';
```

If you read carefully the line that imports the datepicker, you could easily guess that all jQuery UI widgets are under the folder "ui/widgets" and yes, that's correct as shown in Figure 7-11.

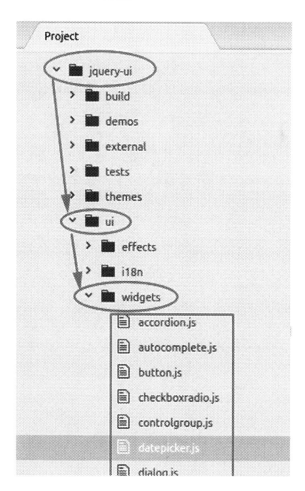

**Figure 7-11.**  *The jQuery-ui widgets location*

Want to use the draggable and droppable widgets? No problem; just add "draggable" and "droppable" widgets like this:

```
// ...
import 'jquery-ui';
// ...
import 'jquery-ui/ui/widgets/draggable';
import 'jquery-ui/ui/widgets/droppable';
```

Pick whatever you like and make sure you have imported 'jquery-ui' before importing any of these widgets.

Now back to the datepicker widget. Is importing the widget's JavaScript file all we need? obviously we will need the related CSS file as well. To find the styling file of any widget, check the folder "themes/base" under "jquery-ui" in node_modules. Figure 7-12 shows the "themes/base" folder where our widget CSS (datepicker.css) is located.

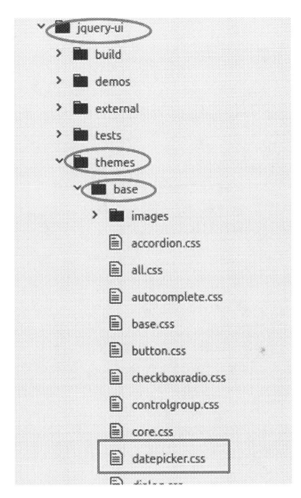

***Figure 7-12.*** *Datepicker.css-related CSS file under jquery-ui/themes/base*

Here we can find the CSS file for each widget separately, or (if you see carefully in the figure above), there is another file called "all.css," which can be used to import all our widgets styles at once. It's up to you to import everything (by importing all.css alone) or to just import the ones you are using in your project, which will reduce the size of your bundle of course.

It's important to note though that while importing "all.css" will bring all the widgets styles, even the ones we are not using (this will make our final bundle bigger in development), thankfully in production mode, webpack will use something called "Tree Shaking," which is a process to get rid of all the unused or unnecessary code. This option is used by default; no need to add anything from your side. So, either you import all the widgets CSS at once using:

```
@import '~jquery-ui/themes/base/all.css';
```

Or import only the one(s) you need, but in this case don't forget to import the theme. css file as well, as shown below:

```
@import '~bootstrap/dist/css/bootstrap.css';
@import '~jquery-ui/themes/base/datepicker.css';
@import '~jquery-ui/themes/base/theme.css';
// ...
```

You may ask, "Where should we place these lines?"

In the "src/application.scss" like we did before, this file will contain all our third-party CSS code as well as ours.

Now that we have imported the necessary files needed for the datepicker widget, let's make it work by adding the following HTML to the template.html file:

```
<input type="text" id="datepicker">
```

After having the input#datepicker element in place, the last thing we need to do is to apply the datepicker() method to that element as follows:

```
// ...
import 'jquery-ui/ui/widgets/datepicker';

$( "#datepicker" ).datepicker();
```

Once done, start the webpack-dev-server if not started:

```
$ npm run start
```

Then let's see if this will work. Open the URL localhost:9000 in your browser and click by your mouse inside the input element. Figure 7-13 shows our datepicker in action.

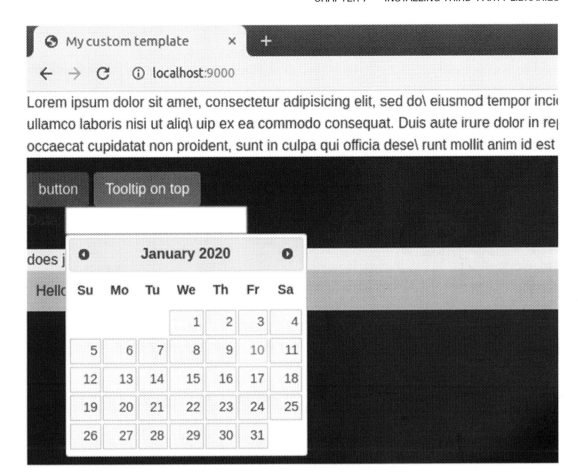

***Figure 7-13.*** *Datepicker opened when clicking inside the input element*

So cool, jQuery UI datepicker is working as expected. All you have to do now is to pick some dates and have fun!

# Installing QuillJS

Now that we have seen how to install and use jQuery and some of its plugins, let's get more familiar with installing more third-party libraries. This time, we will install another JavaScript library called QuillJS. After installing it, you will have a ready-to-use WYSIWYG editor in your web page or application.

The official QuillJS website (`https://quilljs.com/docs/download/`) has a list of the different ways you can use to download the library; in our case we are going to download it via the NPM package manager:

```
$ npm install quill
```

The command above will install the latest version of QuillJS for us. Now if you are familiar or used this library before (if not you can read the documentation), you will know that there are two main files we need to use in order to have this library working.

The first is **quill.js** file, and the second one is **quill.snow.css** (or quill.bubble.css in case you need a flying toolbar that follows your text selection and appears over it).

To get the QuillJS library working, we will use the same principle we used before. We will import "quill.js" in our index.js file, then in our application.scss we will import the CSS file "quill.snow.css." So let's start by importing quill.js in the index.js file as shown in Listing 7-5.

***Listing 7-5.*** Quill JS import and usage

```
import Quill from 'quill';
var quill = new Quill('#editor', {
  theme: 'snow'
})
```

The line after importing quill.js is how we instantiate it. Here we applied Quill to an HTML element with an id="editor" (we will create a div with that id in our template.html), but for now we still need to import the quill.snow.css, so let's open the application.scss file and add the line:

```
@import '~quill/dist/quill.snow.css';
```

How did I know quill.snow.css exists under the dist folder? Well, I just checked manually in "node_modules/quill/dist" and found it as seen in Figure 7-14. All you have to do is import it (do not forget the tilde ( ~ ) we talked about when importing a third-party library CSS).

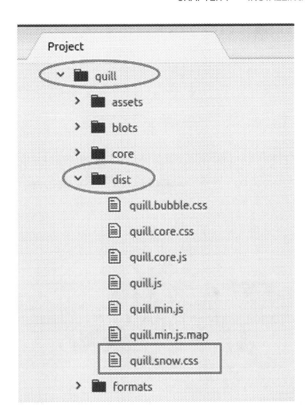

**Figure 7-14.** *Locating the file quill.snow.css file under node_modules/quill/dist*

Let's make sure our WYSIWYG editor is working by adding a div with an id "#editor" to our template.html file. Listing 7-6 shows a little code I copied from the QuillJS quick start guide. The only thing I added is that I wrapped the code in a div with a white background color (#FFF) and added some margin to it as well in order to make Quill WYSIWYG more visible.

**Listing 7-6.** HTML snippet example from QuillJS documentation

```html
<!-- Create the editor container -->
<div style="background:#fff;margin:20px;">
  <div id="editor">
    <p>Hello World!</p>
    <p>Some initial <strong>bold</strong> text</p>
    <p><br></p>
  </div>
</div>
```

Save the template.html and let's start webpack-dev-server using:

```
$ npm run start
```

Open up the browser at `http://localhost:9000` and see that Quill WYSIWYG is working as shown in Figure 7-15.

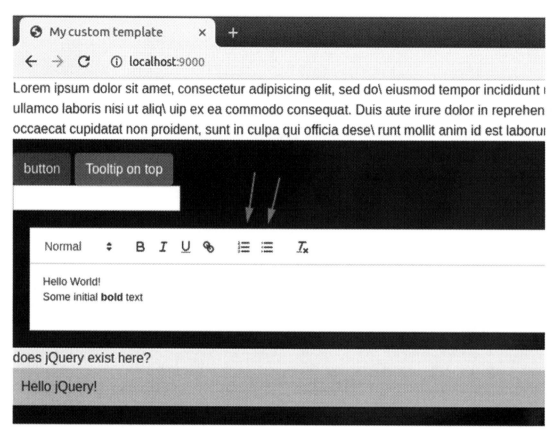

***Figure 7-15.***  *QuillJS wysiwyg interface in action*

Great, QuillJS editor is working. You have just installed QuillJS successfully with a few lines of code.

# Installing CKEDITOR

Let's practice more and install another library. This time we will install CKEDITOR from `https://ckeditor.com/`, which is a popular WYSIWYG editor and largely used on the internet. First, to check if there is any documentation online, go to Google and search for "ckeditor webpack." In order to save you some time, here is the link I found that explains what to do exactly: `https://ckeditor.com/docs/ckeditor5/latest/builds/guides/integration/advanced-setup.html`.

---

**Note**    The reason I'm encouraging you to do the search before installing/using any third-party package is because instructions can be different from a package to another. Even the package name itself can be different than the library name you want to install. Also keep in mind that any link I provide you with to a library's documentation page is subject to change in the future, that's why doing your own search is the best way to go.

---

Let's install CKEDITOR like it's described on the link we found:

```
$ npm install @ckeditor/ckeditor5-build-classic
```

Before going ahead and importing CKEDITOR in the index.js file, let's add a textarea with an id="ckeditor" to our template.html file. That textarea is what we will apply the WYSIWYG to:

```
<textarea id="ckeditor">Some initial text...</textarea>
```

Now, in the index.js file all we have to do is to add some lines of code as shown in Listing 7-7 (which you can find in the Ckeditor documentation) to transform our textarea to a ready-to-use WYSIWYG.

***Listing 7-7.*** Importing and applying ckeditor to textarea#ckeditor

```
// Using ES6 imports:
import ClassicEditor from '@ckeditor/ckeditor5-build-classic';
ClassicEditor
  .create( document.querySelector( '#ckeditor' ) )
```

```
.then( editor => {
    console.log( editor );
} )
.catch( error => {
    console.error( error );
} );
```

Save and start webpack-dev-server using:

```
$ npm run start
```

Then go to the URL `http://localhost:9000` in your browser. Figure 7-16 shows that the textarea was converted to a rich text editor.

***Figure 7-16.*** *Textarea turned to Ckeditor wysiwyg*

CKEDITOR WYSIWYG is functioning, and you can use the same process to install basically any other WYSIWYG editor you want in your project.

# Lazy Loading

Importing third-party JavaScript libraries will make our final bundle bigger. The more libraries we import, the bigger the bundle files will get. Fortunately, in production mode, webpack will get rid of the unused code (thanks to the Tree Shaking), and also our code will get compressed, which reduces the final size drastically ... but sometimes it makes sense to reduce the size even more by relying on some techniques like lazy loading.

The idea behind the lazy loading method is to not load certain libraries upfront, but only loading them whenever we need to; good usage of this is WYSIWYG libraries like the ones we installed previously.

Some WYSIWYG libraries are heavy, and most of the time we need to use them under a specific page(s), so the lazy loading is a perfect solution in this case.

Let's take the example of CKEDITOR that we just saw in the previous section, and let's make it load only if the page contains an element with id #ckeditor as seen in Listing 7-8.

***Listing 7-8.*** Lazy loading the ckeditor library

```
if(document.getElementById('ckeditor')){    import('@ckeditor/ckeditor5-
build-classic').then(function(ClassicEditor){
  ClassicEditor.default
    .create( document.querySelector( '#ckeditor' ) )
    .then( editor => {
      console.log( editor );
    } )
    .catch( error => {
      console.error( error );
    } );
});
}
```

In the code above, we check first if any element in the page has the id #ckeditor. If it exists, we import CKEDITOR, which returns a promise, and then we use a callback function that takes an argument "ClassicEditor," which we will use to turn the #ckeditor textarea to a WYSIWYG.

Make sure to use the property "default" on the passed argument (ClassicEditor) because this is how we get access to the imported module object when the promise is resolved, you can find a notice about this in the webpack documentation as follows.

---

**Note**   When using import() on ES6 modules, you must reference the .default property as it's the actual module object that will be returned when the promise is resolved.

---

That's all it takes to start using lazy loading in your project, and the same principle can be applied to any other library. Just make sure to use it properly and start reducing your bundle size for better performance.

# Summary

In this chapter, we have explored the way to install JavaScript third-party libraries. We have seen the installation and usage of some of the most popular ones like jQuery/jQuery-ui, Bootstrap, QuillJs, Ckeditor. We have also seen how jQuery plugins are slightly different in their importation than other regular libraries; but at the end, I hope you realized that installing and using any library is not too difficult. The installation will be different depending on which one you choose to install. While the principle is similar for most libraries out there, I would recommend that you always check the instructions from the official website (documentation) or the GitHub repository of each specific library.

# CHAPTER 8

# Conclusion

You have made it to the end of this book. I hope it was a fun journey for you and that you have enjoyed every step of it. The goal was really to introduce you to the most necessary things in order to understand how to use webpack in your daily coding, to have a solid base of how things work, and how you can solve problems right away when they occur.

We have seen how to install webpack and how to use the configuration file to make webpack behave the way we want it to. We have seen loaders and plugins and how they are so helpful to add much functionality to our build process, such as how to minify files and deal with caching, etc. Also, we have seen how to alias and resolve our folders, how to use webpack-dev-server to make our development and test loops more efficient, and explored the ways to install third-party libraries in our projects.

We haven't explored all webpack functionalities and tools, but I hope at this point you have more confidence in using webpack, and you have the ability to go and explore more advanced topics by yourself (the web search is your friend, for sure). If you are stuck on anything, then you have the necessary skills to go and ask questions properly in forums like Stack Overflow, etc.

I wish you all the best in your web programming journey, and I would like to hear your feedback about this book as I'm consistently making sure to update it whenever I see a window for improvement. Please feel free to share your opinion/suggestions with me at webpackbeginners@gmail.com.

Best regards,
Mohamed Bouzid.

© Mohamed Bouzid 2020
M. Bouzid, *Webpack for Beginners*, https://doi.org/10.1007/978-1-4842-5896-5_8

# Index

© Mohamed Bouzid 2020
M. Bouzid, *Webpack for Beginners*, https://doi.org/10.1007/978-1-4842-5896-5